Pandemic

for Success

Proven methods to reinvent your sales game when selling to emotionally drained, inbox-dazed, virtual meeting-bored, sales-resistant customers in a pandemic fatigued business world.

By Ryan R. Dohrn

Dedicated to Andre', Ethan, and Dylan for their unwavering support despite Dad being gone all the darn time.

Chapter Index:

Chapter One: The COVID Sales Shift—Reinventing Your Sales Process in a Pandemic Fatigued Sales World

What is pandemic fatigued selling? That phrase alone will make some people lose their minds. What does pandemic fatigued or post-pandemic selling mean? From my perspective, it means selling anything after April of 2020. The World Health Organization (WHO) on March 11, 2020, declared the novel Coronavirus (COVID-19) outbreak a global pandemic. By April 2020, about half of the world's population was under lockdown, with more than 3.9 billion people in more than 90 countries or territories having been asked or ordered to stay at home by their governments. Ever since the lockdowns first began, as active professional sellers we had to change our sales game or risk financial ruin. Sink or swim. Do or die. Crunch or be crunched. The moment of truth. The point of no return.

As of this writing, I am 49 years old. I am a phase 1 COVID survivor. I have been in the sales and marketing business for over 30 years. I have trained and coached over 30,000 sales professionals in seven countries. I have been around the block. And I still sell every day—beyond my business of sales consulting and coaching. If we think things will go back to "normal" once COVID is behind us, we are missing out on several larger points.

1.   Buyers have learned during COVID that they can successfully buy from you over Zoom or GoToMeeting®. From their perspective, face-to-face meetings are not needed. Even though we know we close more when face to face, the new reality is that we will now be conducting more virtual sales calls.

2.   Buyers have learned that they can buy without ever having to talk to us. In fact, 44% of buyers, according to SparxIQ, will determine their product or solution needs without a salesperson. Companies with excellent self-service sales portals sell more than those with a "sales consultant will get back to you" form.

3.   Buyers have lost patience for almost everything—from politics to news to a long sales process. Buyers are more emotional now than ever before.

They want things now. Instant gratification syndrome is real. Good luck with your 10-step Customer Needs Assessments (CNA).

4.   SparxIQ tells us that 70% of buyers will have a defined need before they contact a company to buy a product or service.

5.   Buyers have not been near their desk phones in months. Some companies removed the phones altogether. Those salespeople without cell phone numbers for their prospects and customers learned that connecting via an office phone became nearly impossible. Buyers thus learned that the phone is not an important part of the sales process. We know it is. But, they have learned that they bought during COVID without being on the phone with us.

6.   Price has become the deciding factor, because products often seem similar without a salesperson's intervention.

7.   The relationships we as sales professionals love to develop have often been replaced with transactional selling. Our buyers have learned that they do not have to be our pals to get things done.

If we try to sell in a pandemic fatigued business world the same way we sold before 2020, I assure you that we will be left in the dust by those who are willing to embrace the new buying patterns and change their sales games..

However you want to say it, I think we can agree that COVID-19 forced a dramatic change in our sales organizations. The reason for this book is to help sales organizations manage and implement the changes that will be required to not only survive in a pandemic fatigued sales world, but to thrive, as well. Survival might actually be the first key performance indicator (KPI). But, there are real changes we need to make right now. Changes that can help us thrive and create repeatable patterns of sales success.

What do those changes look like? Finding them will require a certain level of experimentation and fact finding. As much as we have tried to pivot and bend to create profitable sales scenarios in a COVID world, we all ran into and continue to run into problems in our sales processes. One of the bright shining lights in all of this, I've noticed, is that most companies are not simply putting their heads in the sand. They're actually fully aware that they need to do something. They may not know exactly what that is, but they do recognize the need to do something different in a pandemic fatigued sales scenario.

Most companies are set up with either inside or outside sales teams, although there are companies that have both. From my observation, the sales organizations based on an inside sales model have actually done quite well. Their sales challenge has not been nearly as great as that of companies that sell in a more outside-based sales scenario.

For the sake of simplicity, let's assume that your team is one or the other. The main difference is that most inside sales teams have sales leads to work that come from a marketing team. Most outside sellers, like me, do not. We have to cold call and email a prospect to generate business. So, while the first step of your sales process might differ a touch, the rest will be similar. My advice to you: look for the similarities.

As many of you know, I primarily work and sell in the sector of media and digital technology. I had the unique opportunity to win an Emmy while working on the sales and marketing team at Disney. To this end, a lot of my examples will be related to the media business. Do not get lost in the media sales minutia of my advice in this book, though. And do not get lost in the exceptions to what I am sharing. Find refuge in the rules I am sharing. The universal truths. The repeatable patterns of success. I have faith that you can translate my sales ideas into your sales world.

There is a universal dynamic in play in nearly every sales scenario, and it's this: most people do not mind buying, they just hate to be sold. Pandemic fatigued selling accentuates this dynamic. For example, the successful sales process has undergone a shift from pitching to helping. From selling to advising. We have found that the less we sell, the more we will sell.

Simply put, our prospects have lost patience for the long-winded sales process of the past. What are we left with? We can reinvent or we can die by our old-school sales methods in a pandemic fatigued sales and business world.

***

Chapter Two: Is Relationship Selling Dead?

What do the years 1990, 2001, 2007, and 2019 all have in common? These years represent bad times in the American economy. Technical recessions in America. Times when we had to reinvent our sales game and adjust for the circumstances. So, why does the era of selling amidst COVID feel so different? Because unlike other times of economic turmoil, this is one of the first times in American history where the government got involved and shut down business. Then, you add into that the social unrest, political turmoil, and you have a recipe for an emotional sales disaster. Prospects and people in general have lost patience for just about everything. It is a very different climate out there in sales land. The adjustments we as sales warriors need to make to survive will require us to rethink the typical relationship-based sale.

The question I'm often asked is, "Isn't sales all about relationships?" Well, yes and no. Relationships, are they important? Yes, of course they are. But what I'm noticing out there is that if we wait for a relationship to form to sell people something, we're going to be waiting a very long time. We're not going to meet our sales goals. In some cases, the nature of masks and social distancing make it nearly impossible to form new relationships with prospects which are based on personal trust, because personal trust is first born from a visual face-to-face sales appointment. Sure, we can sell via Zoom, but we all know it is just not the same.

I'm not saying that relationships aren't important, or that relationships with a client or a company don't help dramatically. I'm just saying that you don't have to have a relationship with somebody to sell them something.

We are living and selling in a whole new sales world. It's become a lot more transactional out there. Maybe you're thinking, "I don't want to hear that. I hate transactional sales." Well, I do too. I want to have relationships with my clients. I want to be in my clients' weddings, go to ball games with them. It's fun. Selling is fun. It's just hard work. I say it all the time, if sales was easy, everybody would be doing it, and they're not.

So what can we do to be strategic about our thinking on relationship selling and keep things moving forward amidst COVID? Two things, we can move from selling to helping, and get in sync with our clients' emotions.

1-Become a helper

Amidst COVID selling, I'm becoming a helper more than a salesperson, and that's the way I want to be seen by my clients. Would you be surprised to know that now 50% of my sales touches with clients aren't sales related at all? Fifty percent!

I don't confuse customer service with retention. Customer service is expected. If you don't give excellent customer service you're done. Because I'm going to out-sell you and I'll have better customer service.

Retention, on the other hand, is all the things you do beyond the call of duty—and if you're a helper, you'll keep people around for a lifetime. To reiterate, 50% of my sales touches with clients aren't sales-related.

So I might say things like, "Here's an article I found that you might find interesting." Or maybe it's a white paper that I'll share. Or, "Here's a video (make sure it's appropriate) that will make you laugh if you need a pick-me-up today." My favorite is to send lunch to clients at their homes and host a lunch with them.

I'm a helper. Part of being helpful is being prepared before a sales call. To help reach prospects better, I do a great deal of research beforehand, so they know I'm not just some salesperson calling on them in a generic way. Here are some examples: "Hi, Bob. I saw on your website that you do _____. Got a quick second for an idea on that?" Or, "Hi, Julie. I saw on your Facebook page that you guys are promoting _____. I've got a way to help you promote that. May I share an idea with you?"

I want to be the most non-sales salesperson out there calling on them. You've heard me say it before that I've threatened to write a book called "Sell Less to Sell More," because I believe that people don't mind buying things, they just don't like being sold. Change your mindset from "What can I sell them today?" to "How can I help them today?" In the sales world, the idea is to solve a problem—not sell someone something.

2- Get in sync with clients

I like to coach my sales clients that you need to sell the person, not the product. In a pandemic fatigued sales climate, this is critical. You have to understand that there are three kinds of buyers out there. No. 1, there are ego-driven buyers. No. 2, there are emotional buyers. And No. 3, there are logical buyers. Which group do you think is the biggest out there? We did research with over 600 sales reps and asked them which type of prospects they encounter most often. According to our salespeople out there, people like you, the answer was "emotional buyers, over 70% of the time." Yet, what's interesting to me is how many of us sell from a logical standpoint. Like, "Here's our facts." "Here's our readership data." "Here's some stats." Yet, the largest group of buyers out there are emotional buyers. We updated our data and the emotional mindset of sales prospects grew from 63% in 2019 to 74% in 2020.

Remember this: you will sell to others the way that you want to be sold. It's in our DNA. It's human nature. We think we should talk to people the way that we want to be talked to. But sometimes there's a personality mismatch that's going on and the sales rep does not adjust.

Consider that if you're a logical person, you're probably a logical seller. Based on our research, though, you're probably talking to an emotional buyer. So you have to change the way you sell to match that person. How? Emotional buyers love to hear success stories. Sixty-five percent of people will remember a story. Less than 35% will remember stats. If you do encounter a logical buyer in your sales journey, however, go for it. Because logical buyers love data points.

But how do you figure out who the buyer is before you meet with them? Look that person up on LinkedIn or on their other social media accounts. It's so easy to spot them. When you look at my bio description, for example, it says, "I love my job. I love my clients!" Take me for an example … I'm an emotional buyer, therefore, I'm an emotional seller. When you are doing your research, it is easy to spot a person's personality online. But you have to look, and you have to be willing to change the way you approach the sales call. Logical buyers will show lots of lists in their LinkedIN profile. Their posts will be logically based and formatted. Look at the groups they are a part of online for clues. There are clues to a person's personality type everywhere. And, we will explore this more later in this book.

You can also learn about a person's personality when you are talking to them. Do they focus on stats, facts, and data? Well, then you have a logical buyer on your hands. Sell them on the facts. When you tell a story about a happy client, do they respond with a lot of positive gestures? Then Mr. or Mrs. Emotional is in front of you. Keep those data points to a minimum. The real question is, can you adjust your sales pitch on the fly to match that person's personality?

Let's say I'm looking at a LinkedIn profile now. His name is Scott and his profile says, "I'm all-digital all the time." And that tells me that most of the time he's a logical buyer. So when I'm developing my pitch for Scott, it's all about the data.

Is relationship selling dead? The answer is no, it's not dead. It's just changed. If you're going to break through in this tough climate you're going to have to be a helper, not a salesperson. Then, you've got to get in sync with your clients. That means don't necessarily sell the way that you want to be sold. Instead, sell the way that person wants to be sold. I tell people all the time: sell the person, not the product. Relationship selling is not dead. It's just changed. And if you don't change, and if you don't grow, you're going to struggle in the pandemic fatigued sales world out there. But if you keep growing and evolving, you'll continue to be successful in the sales business.

***

Chapter Three: A Fresh New Look At Prospecting

The Top 20 Plan: it's all about perfect prospecting.

Having been in the sales and marketing business since 1996, I can say with authority that I feel your pain! I know what it's like to be a sales executive, where each and every day is not always perfect, and where the act of prospecting has to take a back seat to all the other obligatory tasks. I also had to sell during pre-, mid-, and now post-pandemic. Again, please do not get lost in the fact that you may not personally feel that the pandemic is over. Again, I am not debating that with you. Here is a simple fact, most sales advisors and sales coaches did not sell through the pandemic and have not sold in many years. That is why you need to be very careful about the advice you receive from people who have sold for many years but who aren't currently selling. Think about this ... how could somebody that didn't sell during the pandemic give me advice about selling after the pandemic? The answer is pretty simple. They can't. Most weren't getting rejected and shut down the way we all were. Most weren't having trouble connecting with people like the rest of us. I truly believe this is a valid point, and I'll take some heat for it.

A wise man once told me, you are finally somebody when you've got at least 10 haters. After this global pandemic, very little is the same. As a matter of fact, when I look at my sales process it is now dramatically different after the global pandemic. But that's precisely why you must have a disciplined sales process, and it's why I am writing this book. The process I developed and have taught all over the world, and that I am sharing with you in these pages, is called "The Top 20 Prospecting Plan," and it has been phenomenally successful.

Before we go on, though, let's make sure we are clear on several issues. Prospecting is not as much about selling as it is about getting appointments to sell. Very often, sales people are trying to sell during the prospecting phase. This is a massive error that I see all the time. Prospects don't know you so they certainly are not ready to buy on the spot. There are some products that are sold on the first call. However, in the sales business, most reps will close less than 1% of their sales on the first call. So, each step we walk through in the Top 20 Prospecting Plan is all about getting to a meeting where we can use other new skills to close the deal.

As I mentioned before, even if you represent a great company or product, you are a stranger to the person you are calling on during the prospecting phase. "Stranger danger" is real and it has been ingrained in our minds since birth. So, it is highly likely that a new prospect will be uncomfortable doing business with someone they don't know and trust. Why would they buy from you based on one phone call? This is why prospecting is all about getting to a meeting and not about hard-core selling during this phase of the total sales process.

I like to compare prospecting with working out. If you work out at the local gym once a week, that's great, and it sure beats zero exercise. But if you were to visit your gym every other day, or a couple of days a week, the results and benefits you would receive from having a regimen would be tremendous! As you read through this chapter, think about my analogy of working out, because it really fits my Top 20 Prospecting Plan. Both require repetition, dedication, and discipline to achieve the desired results. And, as with many of the processes and methods I teach, I have broken down the process into smaller steps for clarity and understanding.

The Top 20 Prospecting Plan requires six steps for success:

Step 1: Understanding and working "sales math" to your advantage

Step 2: Defining the perfect prospect

Step 3: Creating your Top 20 list of prospects

Step 4: Working these prospects on the perfect pattern for success

Step 5: Using video to cut through the clutter

Step 6: Creating great prospecting templates to save you time

I am often asked for a step-by-step process to sales success. So in this book, I examine each step in detail in an effort to improve your chances of success.

Step One of the Top 20 Prospecting Plan: Understanding and Working "Sales Math" to Your Advantage

You need a full funnel to be a raging success in sales. Oftentimes in sales training, you'll hear this referred to as "the pipeline." Whatever you choose to call it, you must constantly be working on new prospects. I can share with you emphatically that every time I've experienced the greatest success in my sales career, it was when I had a full hopper of prospects. Yet, I think you would agree that sales success is as much about having good relationships as it is a numbers game. And I believe that these two important components actually go hand-in-hand. You need to be working a lot of prospects actively, and building up a connection with them, if you wish to achieve superstar status with your sales career.

But how do you do this and still manage to complete everything else in your day that must be done? I get it. Each day is not a good day in sales land. Your boss sends you 10 emails that require an immediate reply. The production department needs this or that. I get it. Juggling all these demands makes it absolutely critical to know the "math" behind your sales success, so that you know how to reliably get there. I call this my call-to-close ratio of success, and here's how I figure out that number. Ask yourself these questions:

1.How many prospecting calls do I need to make before I get a meeting with a prospect?

2.How many meetings do I have with prospects before I present a proposal?

3.How many proposals do I present before I close a deal?

This is "sales math" in action. If you're like me, you sat in middle school and asked yourself when all of this math would really help you in life. Well, here it is, back to haunt your very sales life.

In nearly every company I have worked with, the answer almost always starts with a list of 20 prospects. I have run these numbers for companies large and small. Every time, the answer keeps coming back to 20. Your situation may be different. But, for this example, let's use 20. Here is how the sales math commonly works out when you follow my plan. You will need to be working 20 new prospects every 30 days to get eight meetings. From those eight meetings you will present seven proposals. From those seven proposals you will close two to three deals. This is very standard for most sales people I coach. Obviously, over time, you want to improve those numbers, but just imagine if you could close three brand new deals this month. It all comes back to math, and the number that I work from with nearly every account executive I coach is 20.

Now, keep in mind, you are not starting with 20 and then working down to zero. You should always have 20 on your list. After you book a meeting with someone on your Top 20 list, then you can move them from prospect status to in-progress status in your Customer Relationship Management (CRM) tool. And then you place a new prospect on your list to replace the one you just removed.

Your Top 20 is a living document. So again, you will work each prospect on the Top 20 for 30 days using the methods outlined in this chapter. Any person on your Top 20 list who does not respond to you within 30 days will come off the list and is either traded, deleted, or marked as inactive in the CRM.

Now it's time to create your list of 20. So, who are the best prospects to place on the Top 20 list? Let's move to step two.

Step Two of the Top 20 Prospecting Plan:
Defining the Perfect Prospect

Now that you understand that prospecting is the process of getting a meeting with a new prospect, I want to help you understand how to define the perfect prospect. As I work with clients, I frequently hear complaints that their sales reps don't seem to be meeting with the right type of prospects. This is a valid concern, because prospecting the wrong prospects is a huge waste of time, effort, and energy. Sales reps that are new to the business are oftentimes guilty of this practice, but I've observed veteran sales executives making the same mistakes.

Here are seven qualifications that will help you identify a good prospect:

1. They are active in the market or industry you serve.

2. They show signs of need. Perhaps they announce new products with some type of regularity or they open up new branches or offices. A great prospect to have is someone who shows signs of need on a very regular basis. A really awesome tool to help you determine which prospects are showing consistent signs of need is Google Alerts. When Google finds new results such as newspaper articles, blogs, or web pages that match the search terms you've created, Google sends you an email. Google Alerts are as effective as they are easy to use, and they help you monitor your prospects for signs of need.

3. They have a budget. If your prospect is currently active in the market, they typically have some type of budget. What you want to avoid is spending time, effort, and energy with a prospect who has no budget. If they don't have the dollars to spend, the best proposal on the planet won't close a sale.

4. They have bought in the past. You are 60%-70% more likely to sell or upsell a past customer than a new one.

5. They are not a slippery "big fish." Some of you reading this book may actually enjoy the hard sell

because you love a challenge. That's fine if that's your thing. However, while you're chasing after that one crazy elusive fish using your methods, you could be catching tons of other pre-qualified fish using my Top 20 process. Over time, the dollars earned from pre-qualified fish will far outweigh the difficult commission earned from that one crazy fish you just had to catch. That's not to say you should never go after the big accounts, but typically you will have a higher success rate if you avoid prospects that are a hard sell.

6. Does the potential prospect have a social presence online? Do quality research on the prospect. Ok, this one is the last piece of the prospecting puzzle. What information can you find on LinkedIn or Facebook or Instagram that can help you quickly connect with the prospect? I'm not talking about their personal accounts. Let's be honest, mentioning a person's recent trip to Aruba when you don't really know them is flat out creepy. Instead, I am looking for professional information. There really is no reason to blindly cold call anymore because you have so much detailed information at your fingertips. Being relevant during the prospecting process is critical.

7. Do you have the right contact person? If you are calling the operator at a company, you are headed in the right but wrong direction. Use your online tools to find the right person as close to the decision making role as possible.

Keep in mind, each prospect does not have to meet each qualification. But, you need to set a rule for you. For me, if the prospect does not meet most of these criteria, they do not go on my list.

As you're preparing your Top 20 prospect list, keep in mind the seven qualifications of a good prospect, detailed above. Print out this list and put it by your computer. It is ok if your qualifications are different. Create your own list and make it a test for yourself. Don't add a prospect to your prospecting list unless they meet at least three of the qualifications. Don't put anyone on your list that you know absolutely nothing about. If you want outstanding sales success you need to define your perfect sales prospect so that you are truly prospecting the right people.

Step Three of the Top 20 Prospecting Plan:
Creating Your Top 20 List of Prospects

Once you fully understand what makes a good prospect, you're ready to create your Top 20 prospect
list. Use Excel, Word, Google docs, or whatever works
best for you to create your list. Then, you can make
adjustments to the accounts in your CRM tool.

First, create five columns across the top of the page
using the days of the week, one column for each day
of the workweek. Under each column header, list four
new prospect names, for a total for 20 new prospect
names. You'll have five columns, five days, and four
prospects under each day of the week. Now, what
qualifies a prospect as new? New is someone who
has not run or bought from you in the last six months
to a year. If you have a prospect that needs to be re-
newed, you can place them on this list, too. But make
note of this: Many sales reps keep clients on their
prospect lists for years. This is a bad business practice. Hoping that someone will eventually close is
simply not smart. I often write down the 20 prospects
before I enter the prospects into my CRM.

You may also want to categorize and focus each day by an industry or a category. For example, your four names for Monday might all be lawyers. This allows your brain to stay focused on a particular type of conversation while you are prospecting that day. This is not required, but many salespeople find it to be helpful.

Once I am happy with my list and it's been approved by my boss, I add my Top 20 prospects into my CRM tool, or I log in to the CRM tool and tag the correct prospects with "Top 20" so I can manage them. Remember, if the prospect does not meet at least three of my criteria for being a good prospect, then I DO NOT add them to my list. The creation of a quality list is critical. As you are adding them to your CRM tool, do not forget to add in the notes on the CRM. Include your business research plus any shared information you know about them that makes them a great prospect.

Let's cover how you add them to your CRM. Each CRM will handle this differently, but let me give you an example that you may find very useful. With a good CRM, you can create categories for each client, such as lawyers, doctors, or banks. But you can also create a priority or a tag. If you use my Top 20 plan, your priorities will be prospects, in-progress and active. One of the issues I often see is that each and every client in the CRM is marked as active. This will hurt your sales process because you are not able to pull and manage your Top 20 list each and every day with ease. Remember, one of the things I want to do is save you time and reduce your stress. So this type of customization is critical. You can create tags for each client, like Top 20 or maybe your name; I call mine "Ryan's List." This allows you to pull lists within your CRM for sending mass emails, and it's also a great way to better organize your accounts. And better organization, we all know, is critical to our success.

Let me add this in case you're someone who's still holding out on implementing a CRM: nearly every successful sales rep I know uses a CRM tool. And each of these superstar sales reps lives and dies by their CRM tool. One of the secrets to Top 20 success is going to be in the patterns you use to connect with your prospects. Without a CRM it will be almost impossible to keep up with the high level of activity that I am about to coach you through toward sales success.

Step Four of the Top 20 Prospecting Plan: Working These Prospects on the Perfect Pattern for Success

Remember my example about working out in the gym? Prospecting is similar. If you only prospect a client once or twice a month, your results are going to be marginal. You will be very forgettable in the minds of your prospect. If you add in the fact that most salespeople only use email and do not pick up the phone at all, you have a double whammy of bad luck.

To illustrate my point, let's use John from Hillsdale Services as my sample prospect on my Top 20 list. Suppose you contact John from Hillsdale on a Monday and leave a voicemail. If John had a bad day for whatever reason, what is the likelihood of him even remembering your voicemail? What are the chances of him returning your call? Pretty low. You'll be very forgettable. That's why I like to create a pattern of polite persistence when contacting my prospects. I strive to be politely persistent, versus annoyingly persistent—a subtle difference that your prospects will appreciate. I use a combination of voicemail and email touches to get to a meeting with the client. I also use numbered templates to keep my message focused, consistent, and to be sure that I do not say the same thing twice in a row. We will dig into these templates in the next and last step of the prospecting plan.

Here's how the Top 20 Prospecting Plan pattern works: I will call and email John every third business day for 30 days. Yes, every third business day for 30 days. Some of you may be thinking, "Whoa. There's no possible way I'm going to contact somebody that often!" But before you throw this book down, here's a question. Have you ever forgotten to return a phone call or reply to an email from a friend? We all have, and this is a person that you knew and liked.

So, just consider the psychology behind what I am teaching. Since you don't know the prospect you are calling, it will be hard to get a reaction from them because people do not want to talk to strangers. You also need to consider that people are very busy. So 75% are too busy to call us back and 99% do not even know us. What a losing battle, right? No, actually, because we are never going to place someone on our Top 20 list without some type of research to help us cut through the stranger danger issue. If you just share one idea of some way you can help them, or a past connection you both may share, or something you learned about them on LinkedIN, your chances of peaking their interest grows exponentially. Share a quick success story or a competitor's name and you will greatly increase your chances of getting through. (Don't worry. I will share my prospecting templates with you coming up shortly.) The problem I see is that generic salespeople will leave generic voicemails or generic emails and they do this once per month and then blame the client for not replying. But hold on, is this really the fault of the prospect? Think about it.

Here is my formula for success in this phase of the prospecting process:

1.　　If the prospect does not pick up, use voice mail to get a reply to an email. Prospects won't call you back, the vast majority of the time. So why ask them to call you back? Instead, you might say this ... "Hi, Jill. I just sent you an email with the subject line ABC. If you could pop me back a quick reply to that, I would appreciate it. Oh, by the way, this is Ryan over at X. You do not need to call me back. But a reply to that email would be greatly appreciated. Thanks."

2.   Then immediately email the prospect a VERY relevant new idea, success story, and/or a small tidbit of personal data to pique their interest. And remember this: you will increase the likelihood of them opening and reading that email if you follow my rule of three's: three words in the subject line and three sentences in the email. People are busy, so get straight to the point.

3.   Repeat this pattern with a new template every third business day for 30 days. Every outreach must be a fresh, new email with a new subject line. Do NOT resend a re: of a previous email. Each contact should contain a new idea, issue, or other detail. Never leave the same voice mail or send the same email. The idea is to vary your message to prospects in an effort to pique their interest.

4.   They will eventually return your message in some way. You will probably get an email. When they do contact you, move them to a meeting and also to the in-progress status in your CRM. Then replace them on the Top 20 list with a new prospect.

WARNING! One out of 20 prospects will hate this plan. They will hate it. They will email you something like this. "Who taught you this way of selling? Ask for a refund!" I am warning you because many people hate being sold. Most people do not mind buying, they just hate being sold. I can't tell you the number of times I have worked this plan for two weeks and then gotten a reply. People have either returned my calls or left a voice mail and said, "Ryan, thank you for your voice mail—it reminded me that I needed to get back with you." Or, "Oh yeah, Ryan, sorry man I have been so busy. Thanks for checking back with me." People are busy and simply don't have the time to do all the things required of them during the business day.

If you are still thinking there is no possible way that you are willing or able to contact your prospect every third business day, let me provide an example. Dave was a poor salesperson that worked for a very large publishing company. Dave was a really great guy, but he simply wasn't very persistent in his prospecting. He had no long-term success, and his prospecting numbers were very low. Dave was one of those guys who sat in the back of one of my workshops with an attitude of "Nah, I really don't believe in this. I know I'm going to get negative feedback if I use the Top 20 plan of attack." So I gave Dave a challenge. I told him to try contacting his prospects every third day for 30 days; at the end of the 30 days, if his numbers had not improved, I would buy Dave and his wife a steak dinner at the restaurant of their choice. Dave readily accepted my challenge, and for 30 days he contacted his prospects every third business day and used my Top 20 pattern and a version of my templates.

At the end of the 30 days, Dave had more meetings with prospects than he had ever had in his entire sales career! Quite honestly, Dave wasn't that great of a sales rep. But using the Top 20 method, he had a pattern that he could replicate and then repeat. He had found a pattern of repeatable success. Dave is proof that the system works. It creates a pattern, it creates consistency, and it reduces randomness. It really works!

Step Five of the Top 20 Prospecting Plan:
Using Video to Cut Through the Prospecting Clutter

In a pandemic fatigued sales world, it will be more difficult than ever before to cut through the clutter. When I say "clutter" I'm talking about the clutter of people's email inboxes. While we all recognize that the phone is a great way to connect, one that yields powerful results, we can also acknowledge that email is the preferred method of communication by most of our customers. And because we know this and we also know that people watch videos, we can combine the two options to create a winning prospecting scenario—an email that contains a short (two minutes or less) video to entice a prospect to press the play button and learn more about us and why we're calling on them.

While we're on the topic of short, here's another very important point. In my sales consulting, I have found that most emails sent by sales professionals are long and boring. Those sales professionals that are able to embrace short videos as part of the process typically win more meetings. Never forget, the process of prospecting is not about selling. It is all about getting meetings.

Again, very often sales professionals misunderstand this point. If you are selling during the prospecting phase of the sales process, you are selling incorrectly. You'll have plenty of time to sell. This process called prospecting is about getting meetings with customers to sell them things. Selling during the prospecting process will yield you unproductive results. Yes, video can be an excellent way to cut through the clutter at this early stage. For example, I might record a video that says something like this, for example, "Hi, Bonnie, Ryan Dohrn hear from ABC company. I wanted to record you a quick video to explain why I'm calling. We offer a B and C and I would love to share with you how we can save you money, save you time, and ultimately create a winning scenario for your business. Love to connect soon. There's a link below to find a time on my calendar that fits your schedule. Thanks again."

There are numerous tools out there to record yourself and embed the video into your email. If you happen to be a customer using Google Suite email, you can use a tool called CloudHQ to embed video. One of my favorite tools is from a company called Loom, and it is a Google Chrome browser extension. Loom's suite of services for handling video is very detailed and gives the ability to edit and to see who's watched the video, as well. You can even password-protect your videos if that is a concern.

Another tip for using videos is to put the prospect's name on a piece of paper and hold that up to the screen when you start the video recording. That way, when someone sees the preview thumbnail in the actual video, they will know that it's a custom video recorded just for them. I learned this approach from Jason Bay at a company called Blissful Prospecting. He used this technique on me to book a time slot on my Ryan Dohrn Show business podcast. It worked. So, I had him on the show and learned more about it. I thought his method of individualizing the prospecting emails was awesome and it got Justin the result he desired. After all, I replied. In some cases you can use a more generic video that appears to be personalized to get things done very quickly. Now, recording a video for every single customer or prospect is not terribly scalable. But it is something that is important to consider. I believe that personalization is the new currency of marketing. And I believe that individualized customization is the new currency of sales prospecting, as well. In that vein, Chapter ten covers how to set up your computer webcam for video and virtual success.

And now, the last step. What do you say via email? What do you say when you leave a voice mail? Before we jump into templates, I am often asked when is the best time of day to prospect. The answer is normally 11:30 a.m. and 4:30 p.m. Why? Most people do not book meetings at 11:30 a.m. for fear that the meeting will interrupt their lunch. Most people do not book meetings at 4:30 p.m. for fear that the meeting will interrupt their ability to leave at 5 p.m. Keep in mind, though, that every market and industry is different. So test and retest until you find the perfect time.

Step Six of the Top 20 Prospecting Plan:
Creating Great Prospecting Templates to Save Time and Increase Your Chances of Success

Templates are critical to saving time, effort, and energy. When you create your templates, remember that there are four important components of successful voice mails and emails:

1.   They are relevant. You want to include the client's name or product name. Be very specific. "Hi John, I see you're promoting your ABC 300 Model."

2.   They mention a quick story of success. "Your competitor, Rex Reed, has been marketing with us and reported solid success." Or mention a new idea. "I have a new idea for you that could increase your sales."

3.   They promise not to waste the person's time. "John, I pride myself in not wasting people's time. I truly feel this is a great idea for you."

4.   They are short. Remember, prospects are looking to delete your voice mail or email. They are not looking to read or listen. So be brief and relevant.

With these four factors in mind, we can create 6-10 templates that we will use each time we contact our new prospect, whom we'll call Bob. I will share several with you now. Let's go back and think about how to handle Bob on our Top 20 list. On Monday at 11:30 a.m. contact Bob via phone, and leave your voice message and use template 1. Immediately after leaving the voice mail you will send an email that contains the same information. You will then log it into your CRM and set a reminder to contact him in 72 hours.

Following are my Top 20 Sample email/voicemail templates, which are three examples that you can tweak, as needed, and follow. You will obviously need to adjust these for what you sell.

Prospecting Template Example #1: Subject line: XT-200 model

Hi Bob, I saw on Facebook that you are offering your XT-200. I have an idea to help you promote your product and sell more of it. Bob, I feel this idea will be worth your time. Twenty minutes is all I need. Can we meet next week to discuss? I promise not to waste your time.

The voicemail for #1: "Hi Bob. I just sent you an email with the subject line "XT-200." If you could pop me back a quick reply to that, I would appreciate it. Oh, by the way, this is Ryan over at Sinclair. You do not need to call me back. But, a reply to that email would be greatly appreciated. Thanks."

Prospecting Template Example #2: Subject line: Reduce computing time 35%.

Hi Bob, we help companies like ABC reduce their computing time by 35%. Could we meet via phone for a quick chat next Tuesday or Wednesday to discuss? I promise to not waste your time.

The voicemail for #2: "Hi Bob. I just sent you an email with the subject line "Reduce computing time 35%." If you could pop me back a quick reply to that, I would appreciate it. Oh, by the way, this is Ryan over at Sinclair."

Prospecting Template Example #3: Subject line: Short video for you.

Hi Bob, I recorded a VERY short video for you to explain what I was calling about. (Insert the link here.) Ryan

The voicemail for #3: "Hi Bob. I recorded a VERY short video for you to explain what I was calling about. I just sent you an email with the subject line "short video for you" at 11:02 a.m. If you could take a quick look at this short video and pop me back a short reply to that email, I would appreciate it. Oh, by the way, this is Ryan over at Sinclair."

Notice how each voicemail and email message is slightly different from the previous one. Why? There's no reason to repeat the exact message in each progressive voicemail/email that you send, since the contact did not provide the expected response. This method is an ice-breaking technique. You are trying to crack the nut and get a response from a prospect. Whatever you do, and I beg you not to do this, please never use the subject line or say things like I'm calling to check in on you. It is one of the most widely overused phrases in the sales industry. If you want to sound like every other old-school sales dog on the block, use that line. If you want to sound like someone that's progressive and ready to get things done for your new potential customer, try the advice above. And remember, using video is an advanced sales technique, but it's easy to master. I recorded a YouTube video called "How Not to Be a Webcam Zombie." You might want to check it out.

My goal is to create templates that make this process easy to execute. I can contact 10-20 prospects per day with ease. This pattern tells the prospect that you are serious and you are not giving up. Also, by using different voice message templates and different email templates, you are politely persistent in getting to your goal, which is to get a response. There are only two sides to a response, either "Go" or "No." A go might be, "Yeah, give me more information about your offer/product." A no might be, "I'm the wrong person. You need to contact someone else in our company." And sometimes a no is simply that—"No, we're not interested."

What defines a great voicemail and email message and prospecting videos? First and most importantly, your messages should be short, short, short. You would not believe some of the emails I receive from sales reps, messages that are paragraphs long and seemingly endless. I actually cringe when I open one of those emails. So do your prospects.

Another point to consider when sending a business email is the subject line. You already know that business people today get hundreds of emails weekly. Are you aware that over half of emails are now read via a smartphone? Your subject line must be specific and attention-getting. The first sentence of the email should encourage the recipient to open the email, rather than hit the delete button. The last thing you want is to be deleted, so consider your subject line carefully.

Here are several email subject lines that work for me:

1. For your consideration

2. Quick note

3. Quick chat?

4. Five minutes, new idea?

5. Name of their product

6. Short video for you

7. Wrong person?

8. Name of a competitor

9. Bad time?

10. Looking to offer help

The emails and voicemails and videos should never be about you. You will need to create your own templates and test them out on your own. Should you expect your prospect to always answer your voicemails? I don't. But I'm different from a lot of sales coaches in that I actually like leaving voicemails, and I recommend that you do the same. Why? Because leaving high quality, frequent voice messages helps you become a known entity; remember, humans don't like doing business with people they don't know. And contacting your prospect with high frequency helps you advance your marketing message. What about texting? If it works for you, do it. I have found that text messages are not effective in prospecting. But, they are effective in long-term closing deals and client communication.

I still sell to this day. So, as a sales executive, my prospects phone me back approximately 25% of the time, which is better than average. What I see most often is my prospects reply via email. Let's face it, today email is the preferred method of communication for most business people, for a lot of different reasons. It stands to reason that the better you communicate with email, the higher the likelihood of success.

One of the things you can control is repetition—-by having high repetition and quality voicemails, videos, and emails you are being politely persistent. Sometimes we just feel bad about repeatedly calling people. That is why my every third business day pattern works so well. It's just annoying enough to get a response. But I'm not so annoying that it causes people to not want to engage with me. Being politely persistent is you simply doing to someone what they only wish their salespeople would do on a daily basis. You're not doing something that is uncommon or odd. You are doing what a serious sales professional should do on a regular basis. Be persistent enough to get a response.

Let's wrap up this chapter. Remember, there are six steps to the Top 20 Prospecting Plan:

Step 1: Understand and work "sales math" to your advantage

Step 2: Define the perfect prospect

Step 3: Create your Top 20 list of prospects

Step 4: Work those prospects on the perfect pattern for success

Step 5: Use video to cut through the prospecting clutter

Step 6: Create great prospecting templates to save yourself time

Again, just in case you missed this point, we are going to repeat this pattern with a new template every third business day for 30 days. Each contact contains a new idea, issue, or detail. We will never leave the same voicemail or send the same email twice. The idea is to vary our messages in an effort to peak the prospect's interest. Your Top 20 is a living document. You will work each prospect on the Top 20 for 30 days using the methods defined in this chapter. Any person on your Top 20 list that does not respond to you in 30 days will come off the list and is either traded, deleted, or marked as inactive in the CRM.

If a prospect becomes inactive on your list, consider trading some accounts with a peer sales rep. Some sales reps are opposed to trading accounts, I know. Why would you trade your prospects with another sales rep, especially after all your hard work? You know what's going to happen, right? Your peer sales rep will make one call, and the prospect is going to call him or her back! But, if you all trade prospects, the likelihood of the same thing happening to you is very high. Either way, it's wise to give your non-responding prospects a break for 30 days, and then go back to them and try again.

You may be wondering how much time will be required to work your Top 20 list. Once you've developed your pattern, you'll find that it requires approximately 30 minutes in the morning and 30 minutes in the afternoon. If you think you don't have time to work your list religiously, daily, and without fail, you need to make the time! Prospecting is absolutely fundamental to sales success.

Most people don't do it often enough. They don't have a pattern and they don't use a process. I've said it a hundred times, but you need to work harder and be smarter about it.

Again, as a warning, as you work your list you may have a prospect every now and then who will say something like, "Hey Ryan, you are really annoying, calling me all the time." But just because you get one person who doesn't appreciate your tenacity and persistence, don't stop moving forward. Don't stop doing what you need to do in order to be a raging success. I wouldn't insist on you using my process if I didn't know how successful it is going to be for you. I've experienced prospecting success and I've had my coaching clients share their success stories with me. Remember, if sales was easy, everybody would be doing it.

***

Chapter Four: Understanding Buyer Personalities. Connect More to Sell More.

Most salespeople sell the way they want to be sold. Regardless of who they're speaking with, the sales rep continues to sell the way that they want to be sold. For example, you might be sitting with a very logical accountant type of personality. But, if the salesperson is more of an emotional seller, they will sell in more of an emotional way. They are creating a disconnect between themselves and the buyer. The buyer is craving data, stats, and facts. Yet, the salesperson is sharing stories and anecdotes. So, how do we connect better in this new sales world? The answer lies in personality profiling.

Myers and Briggs® is a personality assessment that helps people fall into 16 main personality types. That is a ton of personalities to manage on a sales call. Thankfully in the sales business, though, we can pare that group down to six. From that six, I can isolate that down to three. But you can dig deep on the six, which I will share more on next. Or, you can focus on the main three that we mentioned earlier in the book.

Clearly, we are never going to be able to perfectly match the personality of the person that we're calling on. But it is possible for us to connect with them in a deeper way. The facts are this, more people are emotional now than ever before. You can see it when you observe people talking about politics. You can see it when people are talking about the coronavirus. Emotions are running high across the country. No matter who is sitting in the White House, emotions will run high on both sides of the aisle. I think we all can agree on that. So, as sellers, we have to make sure that we are acutely aware of the situation that is right in front of us. Whether we are on a phone call, a face-to-face sales call, or a virtual sales call. Being aware is half the battle.

Within the group of six personality profiles that I mentioned, there are three main personality types that stand out from the rest. In this chapter we're going to dig into the main personality profiles and then pare them down to the three main personality profiles.

Let's first focus on the three main personality types we mentioned earlier in the book; emotional buyers, logical buyers, and ego-driven buyers. Our research indicates that about 60%-70% of citizens are emotional buyers. About 30% are logical buyers and the rest are ego-driven. It is important as a sales professional for you to be able to pivot and be a mirror to the person that you're meeting with. Meaning, you will speak to them in the way that best suits them, not you as a person. I'm in no way asking you to consider being unethical. Of course, you want to be the person that you are. However, if the person you are stops the total sales process, then you need to change. That is a basic fact of selling.

So, if you know that you are more of a logical person and you like facts, data, and stats, you will need to adjust your sales pitch. You don't want to force a round peg into a square hole. It's just not productive. I've observed, in thirty years of training and working with sales professionals, that most salespeople tend to be a lot more logical in how they sell. That is probably because we love facts and stats to prove our point, especially when we are handling objections from customers. However, knowing that 67% of citizens are emotional, we may need to adjust our pitch.

The essence of selling to an emotional person is selling with success stories. They don't want to be a pioneer. They don't want to be the only person out on the open range exploring new lands. They want to choose trusted solutions, products, and services that others have tried before. They want to know that what they are buying has been proven to produce results. Now, you could use facts and stats to prove your point that results are forthcoming. However, if you're dealing with an emotional buyer, the data and facts are probably going to fall on deaf ears.

When working and selling to someone who is a lot more logical in nature, however, this buyer will want the facts and data to back up their decision to buy a particular product or service. Now, the real question is—what type of person are you? What type of seller are you? What type of buyer are you? You might be saying to yourself, "I think I'm a little bit of both." If that is the case, you are the classic example of an emotional person, an emotional buyer.

In doing research for this book and for various speaking events, I had the opportunity to read numerous articles written by Mary Ellen O'Toole, Ph.D., who is a retired Federal Bureau of Investigation (FBI) criminal profiler. In her pieces, she shares three important points about identifying an individual's personality.

1.   Most criminals do not look like criminals, i.e., "the myth of the straggly haired stranger." Meaning, you can't just look at somebody to determine their personality. You have to dig deeper.

2.   Don't focus on the superficial. Don't get overly lost in what you see. Be sure to do research in advance of your sales calls and try to identify the individual's personality type, based on research.

3.   Ask great questions, listen carefully, and observe. We will talk in chapter 7 about the best questions to ask a client on a sales call. Remember, don't just ask questions to ask questions. Ask questions for a reason.

I feel like we can learn a lot from what the FBI uses as background in profiling criminals, and we can relate that to our sales world. I'm not suggesting that our clients are criminals or have something to hide. I am actually suggesting that superstar salespeople can use some of the same strategies that FBI agents would use to better assess the person sitting in front of them and to connect with that person more deeply. When we connect with individuals in a deeper way, we typically are able to sell to them more efficiently and effectively.

Earlier in this chapter, and in this book itself, I mentioned breaking down six personality types into three basic categories: emotional, logical, and egotistical. Some of you will be fine with just the three main categories, and that's ok. Some of you, though, will want to dig deeper, and I would encourage you to dig deeper. Those three personality types are based on the six main personality types that are often attributed to buyers in the business world. An article by Mike Schultz, President of Rain Group, lays out six buyer personas. I took the three types of buyers from my research, added in context from Mary Ellen O'Toole, and then added Mike's analysis to bring you the context for this chapter. Mike shares the six buyer types as skeptical, decisive, collaborative, relational, analytical, and innovative. Without getting terribly deep into the psychology of the people you're going to be selling to, I do want to walk through these personality types so that you can become more aware and expand your sales game in a pandemic fatigued sales world. After all, we are going to need to shift our thought processes when we're selling to people in this new environment.

Personality Profile One of Six: Skeptical

One of the most common personality types is what we can call Skeptical Scott or Skeptical Sarah. Both Scott or Skeptical Sarah are introspective. This means they are often deep thinkers. Do not confuse introspective with introverted. Those are two different things. Neither Skeptical Scott or Skeptical Sarah will embellish and you should not do so either. This is a very important point because many sales people tend to exaggerate for effect. At least I know that I'm guilty of that. So dealing with someone like Scott or Skeptical Sarah can be a constant challenge. It takes Scott and Sarah a while to develop trust with people—specially salespeople. They don't mind being called a skeptic, either. As a matter of fact, they are very proud of the realism that they bring to the sales conversation.

As you can probably imagine, someone like this falls into the logical or egotistical buying personality category. Because we know that less than 5% of people are egotistical, don't confuse their inability to be emotional with being egotistical. Sometimes when you look at someone like this, you will think they're being egotistical when really, they are just being logical. Since we treat logical and egotistical people differently, as salespeople, don't confuse the two.

So, as a sales professional, what should you say to alter your sales game to better connect with somebody like Skeptical Scott or Skeptical Sarah? Neither are super comfortable on the phone and they prefer to communicate through email. This might be something you point out to a supervisor who insists that you always call them. Don't be unnerved by Scott or Sarah's lack of gestures or feedback. They tend not to be demonstrative one way or the other. Oftentimes they are very hard to read. Their facial expressions might come across as arrogant or confused. In reality, they are probably analyzing everything you're saying. Don't try to get too personal too fast with somebody like this personality type. And, realize that although they may not share much in meetings, you still need to make sure their needs are met. Otherwise, they could quietly block your sale and you may not even know it. This type of personality is a little bit tricky.

Just remember, don't confuse a logical buyer with an egotistical buyer. If you happen to be a logical seller you'll probably be a decent match for them. And because we know that a lot of salespeople are logical, you'll probably be okay with this particular personality.

Personality Profile Two of Six: Decisive

This personality type is what many refer to as "Decisive Diane or Decisive Dan." Their personality profile would fit into the primary category of being "logical." They both solve problems in a decisive, active, and assertive manner. They are proactive, results-driven, and want to win. If you're dealing with Decisive Diane or Decisive Dan, they might seem pushy and overbearing, and may lack tact. They're probably pretty demanding and want things to happen in their way and on their timeline. The real question to ask here is what can we do, say, or alter in our sales routine to best work with this type of client? When you're dealing with someone like Decisive Diane or Decisive Dan, be decisive as well, and demonstrate a willingness to take some risks on your end that can help them succeed. Don't worry too much about conflict that may arise. Conflict does not bother them, and they may even thrive on it. Building consensus is not their natural thing. Not only do they not like the idea of forming a committee, they do not like the word. You want to be on the lookout for Decisive Diane or Decisive Dan and make sure that if you are an emotional seller you change your selling strategy to be more decisive, like Diane or Dan. People typically align themselves with other personalities that fit their personality. I'm in no way suggesting that you lie, cheat, or steal to get the sale. Be authentic. I'm merely suggesting that when you pay attention to a personality type, you can better connect and, thus, should be able to sell more.

Personality Profile Three of Six: Collaborative

The next personality type to look at is what we will call Collaborative Collen or Collaborative Clark. Collaborative Collen or Collaborative Clark like group problem-solving. They are deliberate, diplomatic, and adaptable. They are tactful and respectful. Typically the collaborative personality type fits into the emotional category. As a sales professional the question to ask yourself when sitting in front of Collaborative Collen or Collaborative Clark: What can I do, say, or how can I alter my sales routine to best connect with this person? The answer... help Collaborative Collen or Collaborative Clark build consensus with their team. Work hard to include all the buying influences from their company and maybe your company as well. Facilitate discussions to draw out everyone's thoughts. Don't get frustrated when things take a while. They buy when they are ready to buy, not when you are ready to sell. Because they fall into the emotional group of buyers, if you happen to be a logical seller, be sure to change your thoughts, the structure of your emails, maybe even your slide deck, to best connect with them.

Personality Profile Four of Six: Relational

The next personality type is what many call Relationship Robin or Relationship Rex. Both Relationship Robin and Relationship Rex are very interactive. Social interaction and engagement are important to them. They are enthusiastic, creative problem solvers, team players and, of course, a relationship builders. They like the big picture and are not shy about taking up a lot of your time in discussions. Asking them a question or two will really get them going. Relationship Robin or Relationship Rex both fall inside of the emotional personality group. As a sales professional that's looking to be the best you can be, when dealing with Robin or Rex, keep technical details to a minimum. Make sure you hear their ideas, and share, and stoke their enthusiasm with your own. Robin and Rex will probably weave fairly seamlessly between talking about business and personal matters. If you are a logical seller, this will make you crazy. Don't let it get to you. If you are an emotional seller, don't get too caught up in the off-the-track conversations that may occur. Do your best to keep things focused.

When discussing ideas with Robin or Rex, don't overdo being the voice of reason or reality. What you see as realism, they could see as a real downer.

Personality Profile Five of Six: Analytical

The next personality type we'll examine is what most call Analytical Adam or Analytical Abbie. They both have a deep love for data and that will become clear very quickly. The way things have been done, established methods, and data are all important to Analytical Adam and Analytical Abbie. So it takes a lot of time to process the data you're going to present. Be patient. Be ready for these delays.

Be cautious, because they both follows rules, procedures, and established standards. They are comprehensive problem solvers because they examine problems from every angle. Analytical Adam or Analytical Abbie are fairly easy to spot, and they will need a lot of your data and statistics. Your success stories will almost assuredly be meaningless to somebody like them. If you're an emotional seller, you are going to be a 100% personality mismatch for them in so many obvious ways.

So pay attention when you run into Adam or Abbie. If you're going to adjust your sales game to be a raging success, you need to be able to spot an Analytical Adam or Abbie from a mile away. They might even require a different slide deck that is filled with data points. As much as you may not want to hear this... they could care less about your stories. They could care less about others that have done great things, unless they are inside their organization or someone that they feel is a peer. With somebody like Al or Abbie, you'll need to provide the backup data to help them make an appropriate decision. Appropriate detail will be important, and detail appropriate to them is what's most important. Make sure that you asked them what type of data they need. In some cases their insistence for things can come off as being arrogant. Be sure to get very specific information on what information they will need. In addition, be careful, because if you push Adam or Abbie too hard before they have completed their analysis, you may find yourself and your sale blocked.

There is a cautionary tale about dealing with somebody like Adam or Abbie. At some point, because they can occasionally leave the data door open way longer than it needs to be, you might need to push back a little. But take special care not to criticize their process. Here is where stepping up your sales game is mission critical.

Personality Profile Six of Six: Innovative

There is one final personality type to pay special attention to, and some like to refer to this personality as Innovative Irene or Innovative Isaac. They could care less about your rules, procedures, and how things have been done in the past. Innovative Irene or Innovative Isaac will become very frustrated when you try to share with them how other people have done things. Their response to a success story is probably going to be negative. They are both going to be floored that you'll be comparing them or their company to somebody else. Both consider themselves to be cutting edge. Innovators who develop ideas and strategies independent of rules and what other people think. They are both going to be your classic egotistical buyer personality. But, they will try to marry that personality with some logic. The reason they will do this is because most people respond negatively to egomaniacs. So they use data to back up their ego. Both are informal and solve problems creatively. Boundaries are for testing, pushing, and crossing, according to Irene and Isaac. They are both difficult to prospect unless you have some type of mutual connection. That could be as a business acquaintance or as a fellow alumnus. Be careful about name dropping. They truly feel that they are the smartest person in the room, and they will be surprised when their ideas aren't loved by others. This personality is a hard one to sell to, so consider what you will change in your sales game to better connect with someone like this.

With personality types like Innovative Irene or Innovative Isaac, I like to brainstorm with them. I like to stoke their ideas for new ways of doing things, and I like to flatter them for their ability to come up with new ideas. I don't see this as being unauthentic. Rather, I see this as sales strategy. For example, when you set the agenda for the meeting, make sure that you are willing to change that agenda to meet their needs. As a matter of fact, when I start meetings with people like this, I normally say something along the lines of, "What direction would you like our agenda to go today? I was thinking of covering these three things. But, I'm happy to alter my agenda to meet your specific needs."

Don't shut down creative talk. Keep it moving forward because Innovative Irene or Innovative Isaac can often be on the disorganized side. Be prepared to jump all over the place. They will become frustrated when you try to make them follow your slide deck. Show how working with you can bring their ideas to reality. Don't argue much. They both much prefer somebody that just says "yes" to their ideas. Be careful about pushing back too hard. Be careful not to be a big downer or to beat the drum about certain points. Get on board quickly with Innovative Irene or Innovative Isaac or you will lose the sail.

So, why dig so deeply into personality? You can either dig deep or you can focus on those three main personality types: emotional buyers, logical buyers, and egotistical buyers. If you're looking to take your sales game to the next level though, I would encourage you to extensively research the wider range of various personality types laid out here. Once you get good at selling to different personality types, you will simply sell more. Some people come by this fairly naturally. They are able to mirror the person they are talking to and can see the benefits right away. Others have to really spend time observing and figuring this out. In advance of a meeting how would you know what type of person you're dealing with? You do research and you look for clues.

I'm able to find out a lot about most people on LinkedIn or social media prior to a meeting. When you're on LinkedIn and you see someone making a lot of lists in their summaries or talking about data, you can most assuredly see that they are a logical buyer. When you see in people's profiles that they "love their job" or they are the "king of fun times," that most assuredly leads you to understand that they are more emotional in nature. You can also look at the titles and jobs that people have had to determine which type of jobs they typically gravitate towards. Looking at those job types will probably tell you what type of personality type aligns with this person. Also, look at people's recommendations on LinkedIn. Very often those recommendations will reveal personality types, as well.

Yet another LinkedIn tip is to specifically look at what groups people are part of. This will give you some gentle understanding of how they might think, as well. When you stalk people on social media, however, be careful not to mention that in your meetings. What you find on LinkedIn is professional and can be shared. What you find on Instagram or Facebook is normally too personal to be shared in a meeting. Trust me on this. You don't want to come across as creepy. Use the data to your benefit, but don't make it a big part of the meeting.

For example, if I can see on Twitter or Facebook that someone is sharing a lot of stories about data, then I can only make the assumption that they like those types of articles and that they are more of a data-driven person. That would put them into the logical buyer pool. Many people ask me ..."Ryan, is it really this difficult to sell?" The answer is yes. Most people don't mind buying things, they just hate the prospect of being sold. So as an unintended consequence, they typically don't like salespeople either. There have been numerous studies documenting that most buyers would rather go to the dentist then talk to a salesperson. That is very sad. Most of us are in this profession to help people and to make money. But most of us do love helping our customers. We love to see our customers succeed. So it is sad to learn that most citizens think of salespeople as sleazy or slimy. That is just not who we are.

Yet, we do have a very tough job. But the more we learn, the more we will grow. And the more we grow, the better sales reps we become. So on my growth journey as a salesperson, personality profiling is something that has become a bit of a personal passion for me. I truly enjoy digging in on the psychology behind people. And as a result of this, I sell more now than I've ever sold before and I truly believe it's because I connect with people more deeply as a result of doing this research. This was one of my secrets of selling during the global pandemic. My sales training clients that I worked with before the pandemic have reported that they could see the technique benefitting them, as well.

As I'm known for saying, if sales was easy, everybody would be doing it. But it is a hard job. It requires a lot of research and preparation. I would deeply encourage you to consider all these personality types and, if nothing else, just try to put your different prospects into the three main personality pools. I have observed that salespeople that connect more deeply with their prospects will typically sell 45%-55% more than those who do not try to connect in a deep way with their clients or prospects.

***

Chapter Five: Don't Be A One-Trick Sales Pony

In this chapter I will be explaining the marketing triangle of success. As I mentioned in chapter one, I sell mostly in the media and digital tech space. For those of you that do not sell in this space, please translate these ideas into your specialization. I always like to hear about other sales scenarios from outside my industry. I hope you will as well. Learning from others is super important.

The idiom one-trick pony is derived from the circus. A circus featuring a pony that has only been trained to perform one trick and often is not very entertaining. Unfortunately, that is how we are often seen in the media sales business. All too often advertisers see us as being good for only one thing, bringing them new business. While this is an important part of what we do, it is not the only thing that we do. It is critical as media sales professionals that we recognize this is a problem and we deal with it head-on. Whether in prospecting or hosting meetings, I always am talking with potential and current advertisers about the marketing triangle of success. If I could be so bold, I would like to lay claim to that phrase here in this book. I believe that an educated Advertiser will always buy more media for me. When I am teaching my ad sales training workshops I tell media sales pro's like all of you, that you need to think more like a teacher than a salesperson. What am I teaching? The marketing triangle of success.

The marketing triangle of success has three sides. This is a formula that has been followed for years by larger, more sophisticated companies. But, if we teach it to our clients, I believe they will spend more money with us. On the bottom of the marketing triangle is new business development. On one of the other angles of the triangle, is re-engagement with past customers. On the other side of the triangle, is retaining customers. All three of these components of the marketing triangle of success are things that we can help an Advertiser control. But, if we don't explain this to them, they truly will not understand why this is important. The triangle is actually the strongest geometric shape.

When engineers build structures, they want to make sure that the structure can bear weight. In other words, they do not want the structure to fall down when a force is applied to it. For example, bridges must be able to hold up the materials that make the bridge, as well as all of the traffic traveling across it. That is why you see many bridges built out of series of connected triangles. When a force, the load, is applied to one of the corners of a triangle, it is distributed down each side. That is why it's a great shape to use in describing how we can be helpful to our clients via their advertising. Let's break down each side of the triangle.

On the base of the triangle and in every graphical representation that you create, should be new business development. It is foundational. All advertisers want new business coming through the door. That new business comes in various shapes and sizes, but we impact it none the less. But, if we don't explain the other sides of the triangle we are seen as the proverbial one-trick pony. New business development is top of mind and foremost to every Advertiser. When we talk about new business development, I also talk about managing expectations. I like to ask questions like, "What does one new customer mean to you?" Or, I like the question "If we could help you bring in even one new customer what would that mean to you?" Or, "When this ad campaign runs perfectly what type of results would you be looking for?" All these questions lead to managing expectations and setting up your Advertiser for success. Not asking these questions will put an unfair expectation on you as the media company. Please keep in mind that as much as I love my advertisers, most of them, they are some of the most unrealistic individuals that we will deal with. They literally feel that they can spend $500 with us and they will get $500,000 in return. That's okay. We know this. So, we should be prepared to work with it. Explaining the foundational base of the marketing triangle of success is important but you have to marry that with the management of customer expectations as well.

New business is the base of the triangle, but one of the other sides of the triangle is customer engagement. It's important for us to explain to an Advertiser that re-engaging with past customers is a mathematically positive equation that they should dedicate some marketing dollars to in order to maximize the return on investment from the total marketing plan. Experts tell us that you are 60%-70% more likely to re-sign or re-engage with a past customer. This applies to your Advertiser and it applies to you as a media sales professional as well. Yet, most business owners and companies do not dedicate any budget to re-engagement or renewal of previous customers. When the focus is always on new business development, experts tell us that you are only about ten to 15% likely to close a new account. So, knowing these mathematical statistics, it would only make sense for The Advertiser to focus a little bit of the budget on re-engaging or renewing past customers of theirs. Very rarely do I come across an advertiser that does not want to re-engage with past customers. But, they are so focused on new business development, an important part of the marketing triangle, that they often forget to dedicate any budget to re-engaging former customers. If we don't point it out, we'll never get money for it. A lot of what I try to teach my media sales training and coaching clients is that we need to think like a teacher and not so much like a salesperson. Explain it to sell it.

The other side of the triangle, still very important, is customer retention. This should be important to you as a sales professional and it should be important to all business owners and companies out there. Yet, again, I see very infrequently, budgets dedicated to retention or thanking their customers. This is a conversation that many people would frame as a "branding." Just the nature of the word itself branding often means to an Advertiser that they will run an ad with us and not expect any results. That is why I have changed how I speak about branding. I have now begun speaking in terms of "brand maintenance." I'm not trying to play semantics here with you. Brand maintenance and branding are the same thing. But, what I've noticed, is when I throw the word maintenance into the word sequence there is an implied value that is received. When you maintain your vehicle or perform vehicle maintenance you're receiving something for the price that you pay. It's a subtle and small change but something that can be pretty darn dramatic. Again, if we do not explain this side of the marketing triangle of success, how can we expect to get paid for it? We can't. Each side of the triangle is important. I will say to the advertiser, "You have spent thousands of dollars getting your business to where it is today. How about we dedicate some marketing dollars to protecting your turf and protecting your brand? Let's look at some brand maintenance activities."

The marketing triangle of success is only as good as your ability to explain it. Because every sales professional hates role-playing, it's important for us to figure out the best way to present this concept. It's also important for us to have good success stories and examples of other advertisers that truly do follow the marketing triangle of success. In my opinion, the only way to effectively do this is with a nice graphical presentation. Experts tell us that over 70% of what you learn is taken into your brain through your eyes. That's why I like to include a slide that shows the marketing triangle of success in every presentation. I like to walk my advertisers through what it looks like and speak about each side of the triangle. Many times I'll do this by drawing on a piece of paper or having some type of graphical representation in my slide deck. If I'm face-to-face I prefer to draw it on a piece of paper. This allows me to create better engagement with the advertiser. And, in addition, to this show and tell, I can also further draw on each side of the triangle as we talk about budget allocation. I am a fan of drawing things out on paper or with my virtual pen inside Zoom® or whatever system you use for virtual meetings. We will talk more about hosting great virtual meetings later in the book.

Being a one-trick sales pony does mean that you do at least have one trick. I suppose that is always a place to start. But expanding this conversation will help you get more advertising dollars. As I said previously, I truly do believe, that an educated Advertiser/Client, will spend more money with you. Once you wrap your mind around this concept you will begin to get out of sales mode and move more into educator mode. A study a few years ago by the consulting company SAP told us that 89% of buyers would rather go to the dentist than talk to a salesperson. You've heard me talk about this on my podcast many times and previously here in the book. If this is indeed true, this is a bit scary for all of us. So, that's why I feel that the epitome of consultative selling is explaining the marketing triangle of success. Never forget friends, and I say this all the time, if sales was easy everybody be doing it. And they are not. We are the chosen few. We have found a career that will feed our families for a lifetime! We just need to keep growing... always in all ways.

***

Chapter Six: The Death of the Customer Needs Assessment?

As we navigate the changes in our world right now, I think it's important to focus on the Customer Needs Assessment (CNA).

If you're in a leadership role, right now you might be saying, "No, Ryan, don't talk about <u>not</u> doing a CNA." Hold on.

Here's my point, though. We're living in a world where people are mostly certainly limited on patience. For the most part, I think everybody right now is actually limited to some degree in their cognitive abilities. People are tired. So how do we expect someone we're selling to to actually understand what they need vs. what they want?

Think about this regarding the Customer Needs Assessment. Very often it focuses in on what they want, and not what they need. Think about all the questions you ask. "What's your budget?" "What are your goals?" "What keeps you up at night?" "What's the biggest business challenge for you?" "How can we help you overcome that?"

It's all focusing on what they want. They want paying customers, they want new business, they want to retain business. Want, want, want.

It really should be called the Customer Wants Assessment, right? Think through this with me before you shut down on the idea. Be open-minded. I sell every day, just like you do. I've been in sales and marketing for 30 years. I didn't stop selling to become a consultant; I love the sales business.

So here's a radical idea: Maybe we need to find our joy in that, in the sales business.

So this Customer Needs Assessment, where we ask them what they need—it really focuses on what somebody wants. So if we don't actually guide them toward what they need, they're going to come back to us in the coming weeks or months and say, "I didn't get any ROI." They didn't get the return on investment that they needed. And so a lot of the time they didn't get what they <u>needed</u> because we gave them what they <u>wanted</u>.

So here's what I want you to consider in addition to the CNA: putting forth powerful recommendations.

Let me give you some background on my thoughts here.

There are a lot of impatient people out there right now. How many of you feel cranky right now? I feel cranky. I'm cranky about the world, I'm cranky about politics, I'm cranky about COVID. I'm just cranky. And it's difficult to deal with cranky people you're selling to. They try to tell you what they want, and you're trying to convince them what they need, so I'd like to talk to you about recommendations instead.

Were you aware that Nielsen, the TV ratings and audits company, reports that recommendations are the most trusted form of information? This is a tool we can use as salespeople, and this is something I stress in my sales training. We can coach our customers on why they need something, and what they need to buy. And then we can get them to a point where we not only fulfill their wants, but we actually get to the heart of what they need.

Harvard Business Review had a review of 600 top sales professionals, and here's what they found out: Most sales reps rely on a customer to coach them through the sales process. The superstar sales reps that I work with, we coach the customer. We know the questions we need to ask the customer to find out what it is they truly need beyond what they want.

But still, most customers are going to struggle to identify an exact need. For example, they might say, "I need more customers." So I may say, "When you say 'customers,' can you be more specific? Tell me more. Give me some detail about that."

So, to guide customers to a recommendation, I'm doing a great deal of comparative selling.

Creating a comparative conversation helps you draw out ego, helps you draw out emotion, and helps you draw out logic.

Sometimes in the advertising business, where I spend a lot of my time, I'll say things like, "Who do you feel does a great job of marketing here in our community?" I suppose they could say, "Nobody does." But typically they give an example of somebody.

And then I'll say, "Do you want to be like them, better than them, less than them? Do you want to be competitive with them, or do you want to dominate them?" I work to determine what's the circumstance for them.

What I don't ask them is what their budget is. Because if you ask them what their budget is, they're probably going to give you a number based on their reality. Not the reality of marketing in the community where you live.

My next tool to guide customers to a recommendation is sharing success stories through comparative selling.

Let's say, for example, that you sell in the software space. When you create a comparative conversation, you're actually comparing the customer that you have on the phone to other customers that you've had in the past that are very, very happy.

Here's an example. When I sell, I ethically share stories about my current clients. I share what they love about me, what they love about the software, what they've loved about the company, what they've loved about the experience—and I can begin to compare customers.

I use these comparative conversations so I can recommend products based on the happiness of other customers, realizing that other customers' happiness will oftentimes translate to the happiness of this new customer that I'm trying to get.

It's easy—and it's all about sharing success stories.

But sometimes we salespeople don't like to do this, and the reason we don't is because we feel like we're talking about a customer behind that customer's back. But we're not. What we're actually doing is shouting from the mountaintop how happy other customers are with us.

And if they're happy, then this new customer probably will be, too. And happiness is ultimately what we're seeking.

Now, you might get really technical about this, and you might say, "Well, Ryan, I'm not looking for happiness, what I'm looking for is making sure they have the ROI that they demand." But I am here to tell you, when push comes to shove what most people want to do is what others have done to be successful.

Just last weekend I was talking with a friend of mine. She said, "I'm having some great luck losing weight." I said, "Cool! I would love to drop 15 pounds. I think it would make me happy and make my wife happy. What are you doing?"

And she told me about her weight management plan. So I immediately went home and looked it up online to find out how I could get involved in this.

The point is, her success story led me to make a great buying decision, for me. This is a simple buying example, but it can resonate through everything you do.

Consider that when you have a linear conversation, a one-way conversation with a client, what you do is keep them inside their own bubble. And it's not until somebody gets out of their bubble—OUT of it—that they realize, "Oh, other people out here are happy, they're being successful, and I want to be like them. What are they doing? What is their weight loss plan? How did it work for them? What made them happy?"

As a salesperson, if I can help customers be happy—happy like other people—then all of a sudden, they start buying what it is that I'm selling. It's a simple sales concept that works and that resonates with customers.

I've had the opportunity to walk through and be a part of almost every sales training program in America, from Carnegie to Sandler. And a problem I see is that they focus on a one-way conversation where you identify somebody's pain and then you fix that pain.

That's great in theory, but as a salesperson you can actually take it to the next level by telling them about other happy customers whose pain you have eliminated. It's about proving that you have done something for other people.

It's about getting beyond the old-fashioned Customer Needs Assessment to start recommending products, sharing success stories, and creating comparative conversations.

And remember, in these conversations, be mindful of the questions that you ask. Make sure those questions take you to a better place.

So, what are the questions?

I try not to ask the same questions that have been asked for the last 10-15 years, the ones that make you sound like all the other salespeople that have shown up either face to face, on Zoom, or on the phone.

I strive to ask the questions that other salespeople don't. In that vein, I don't ask, "What keeps you up at night?" I would rather ask a question, something along the lines of, "If we could help bring you one perfect customer, what would that customer look like?"

Or, "When you agreed to meet with me, was there a business challenge you were hoping that I could help you solve?"

I'll say it again, rather than asking, "What's your budget?" ... especially in the sales world where I spend a lot of my time in the advertising business, I'll say, "If we could help you be bigger and better than your nearest competitor, what would that look like?" "In the past, what have you done to solve these types of problems?"

Or I might use something back from my good old Sandler days like, "What is the biggest challenge that you're facing right now that you think I can help you solve?" Or "How long has that been a challenge or a problem for you?" "What have you done in the past to fix that problem or remove that problem from the greater equation of your business?"

When you ask your questions, remember these ideas I espouse in my sales training programs: Most people want to be led. Most people like recommendations. Most people don't like a linear conversation—they want to know what others are doing and what you have done to help other people.

So, in closing, the Customer Needs Assessment isn't dead, necessarily, but if we don't breathe some new life into it, if we keep doing the same thing we've always done, we're going to get the same result. If we want to see a different result, we've got to do something different.

That's why we're advisors … try to be an advisor, don't be a salesperson. Breathe some new life into your Customer Needs Assessment.

And managers out there—sales directors, sales leaders—look at the questions your salespeople are asking prospects and customers. Make sure that they're updated. Make sure they reflect the current situation that we're in. Now, let's dig in on those questions in the next chapter.

***

Chapter Seven: Stop With the Old-School, Open-Ended Questions, Please

A recent sales call where I was being sold began like this, "Hey Ryan. Thanks for the time. I would like to start by you telling me about your company?" I said, "What do you know already?" The salesperson said, "Ummm… not much and that is why I asked."

Can you tell the intelligence or how prepared a person is for a sales conversation based on the questions that they ask? I believe the answer is, YES! Now, what are the best questions to ask? Before we get to that, I think we all have to wrestle with the decision to potentially ask better or different questions than we've been asking for years. We're probably going to have to change our sales game a little bit. But, after all, that's what this book is all about—making over your sales game. If I've heard it once, I've heard a thousand times … Never ask a question that a prospect can answer with the word "yes" or "no." Standard open ended questions, right?

That is all fine and dandy, as long as you're asking the right questions. I feel like there are several things we should be thinking about in this chapter. The first is making sure that we are asking the best questions we can possibly ask, and asking questions that have not already been used by other sales reps for years. And the second is asking questions that help us differentiate ourselves from other salespeople. In most sales scenarios, " sales gurus" will tell you that you have three objectives when asking questions. Finding out budget, buying time-line, and if the person you are taking to is the decision maker. While I see this importance I would consider the questions you need to ask to get these answers to be three of the worst questions to ask. But, I'll list them here just to create a point of clarity. The first question, what is your budget? Bad. I'll explain why in a second. The second question, are you the decision maker? Bad. I'll explain more in a second. And the third question, what is your timeline for making a decision? Again, bad. I'll explain more in a moment, but all of these questions have been well-established in sales business books since 1985. I like to jokingly tell people that the 1980s are calling and they want these questions back. At face value, there's truly nothing wrong with these questions. I just feel that in a pandemic fatigued selling scenario, we need to be better than these questions. Why? Because, if we keep doing the same thing over and over again and expecting a different result, we are continuously trying to redefine insanity. I think we all could agree that insanity does not need a new definition. Just to stop the emails from coming my way, I fully recognize that clinical insanity is much different than sales insanity as I am defining it. As sales people, the answers we need from the above three questions are important. However, let's ask those questions in a way that shows our prospect we are a modern seller with a focus on saving them time, effort, and energy. My biggest concern with questions like this is that you are typically selling to someone who has been asked these questions a thousand times. So, you come across as being a typical salesperson. I think we have well-established in this book that we don't want to be "typical" Our goal is to be extraordinary. Our goal is to be different. Our goal is to move the conversation forward, faster.

Now I'm going to give you the 15 questions that I most often ask. But let's be clear, I'm not going to ask

15 questions on every sales call. In fact, very rarely do I ask more than five or six questions. But, because each of our selling situations is unique and different, I want to list them all and you can determine which questions fit best for your sales scenario. I'm in no way suggesting that you remove asking questions from your sales process. As a matter of fact, I clearly and unequivocally state that that would be flat-out crazy. I just want all of us to be better than the next sales executive that will call on a prospect. My concern is that if we all ask the same questions in a pandemic fatigued selling situation that we did before the pandemic, we will be seen as the same rep that sold pre-COVID and nothing has changed. A recent blogger actually suggested that salespeople just ignore that COVID ever happened. Really? Come on. We are all better than that.

1.   When you decided to meet with me today, what problem were you hoping that I could help you solve? I think this is a great question to ask—great way to start a conversation. I feel that most people want us to cut to the chase and get to the point. A lot

of time is spent in soft selling and building rapport, and I think that's absolutely fine. But be careful that your rapport-building doesn't come across as being a waste of time. Now, you might be in a situation where you're cold calling somebody. This is obviously not the question you would ask in that situation. Most of the questions that I propose here are questions you would use on a sales call where you have a verified appointment with a customer, or when a customer has asked you to call them.

2.   (Referencing question #1) How long has this been an issue for you or the company? Or, was this an issue before COVID? This is an important question to ask in this sequence of the first three questions because you want to identify how long this client has been experiencing discomfort, dissatisfaction, or pain. Lots of different sales training programs talk about identifying a customer's pain points. This is actually the purpose of this question. Now, keep in mind you're not the first salesperson to ask this sequence of questions. So, be aware of the facial expressions you see and the response that you get.

3.   (Referencing question #2) What have you done to try and fix or resolve this issue in the past? Be careful not to ask the sequence of questions too quickly. You don't want it to sound rehearsed. Be soft about it. Make sure you come across as being genuine and understanding. Most often, these three questions are a sequence. But, they do not have to be. The goal of the first three is to identify the client's pain and then propose how you can remove the pain. As we move to question four, we are moving away from the first three question sequence. Again, I am not saying that there is an exact order to the rest of these questions.

4.   How does your company evaluate new ideas and solutions from companies like ours? This is the question that I most often ask that is critically important. I truly believe that managing expectations from the very first encounter is part and parcel of your long-term success as a sales representative to this client. This question is very much like the question about timelines. But, it is said in a different way. As you look at these questions, if you feel like you have been asking these already, I would suggest that

maybe you are on the right path for success. But, as you look through these questions you'll probably find some new ways to tackle approaching questions and answers with your clients.

5.   What is the biggest challenge/goal/objective for your company in the next six months? (You could use the same sequence as shown in #1) Be cognizant of the fact that this question can lead to some good discussions, but it can also get you off track and take you into the weeds. Be careful about that. This may not be a question you need to ask on a regular basis, but there are times that it will be useful, and you'll need to make that determination. Remember, we don't ask questions just to ask questions. Ask every single question with a purpose.

6.   Fast forward to the end of this project. What does the ideal outcome look like for you or for your company if you were to engage with us? This is another question about managing expectations. You don't have to say it exactly like this. You can make it your own. But, it is an important question to ask.

7.   What do you like or dislike about your current solution provider? (Or, whatever is applicable to your

selling situation.) This question can be a little bit tricky at times. You want to be careful not to talk negatively about your competition or other providers in your category. But, when you can find out what they don't like about their current provider you can often bring them over to your way of thinking very, very quickly. Now, one thing on this particular question, is to be careful that you don't come across as being the person that can solve every single problem that a customer has. Transparency is important. But know that if you're seen as somebody that's willing to say "yes" to anything, that can backfire as well.

8.   What would I need to do to earn your business for a lifetime? This question is more about retention then it is about managing expectations. It is not the best question on every single sales call. But I like to use it on a regular basis. I like to say to people that their long-term satisfaction is my priority. Oftentimes, I also ask people if they are satisfied, can I can count on them for a referral, which is a vital part of my business. I want them to know that I'm not a flash-in-the-pan salesperson that's going to sell them something and then be gone. That's an important part of the

puzzle, you explaining that you're not going to sell them and then pass them on to somebody else. Now, if your company is set up that way, you may need to rethink your pandemic fatigued sales process. Maybe create a hand off sequence that does NOT make the new client feel like they are being dropped off at the first day of Kindergarten.

9.   Based on past experiences with other providers, what is that one thing we could do wrong that would really hinder our success together? Transparency is key. This question helps you find out about the things that might make the new client crazy. Things that might take the project off track if they occur.

10.   What do you feel is your company's greatest strength compared to others in the same category? With this question you want to make sure you don't come across as being unprepared. You might want to start the question by saying something like, "In an effort to get to know your company better ... What do you feel is your company's greatest strength?"

11.   If we could help you bring in one new customer what would that customer look like? ("Could you be

specific?" Or, "What is one new client worth to you?")
Identifying the value that you're going to bring to the
client in selling them your product or service is critical. Many customers are solely focused on their return on investment matrix. This is one of the easiest
ways to figure out a solid path to ROI.

12.   How has COVID impacted your company? This
question can open up all kinds of different discussions. Because each of us is selling something different, I suggest making this question more specific to
the industry you're working in, as well as making it as
specific as you can. For example, if I was selling in
the media business, I might say something like, "How
has your marketing program been impacted by the
current pandemic?"

13.   Are there any new products or services that
you will debut in the next six months? This question is
different than the one I wrote about above. This is really about long-term strategic planning. Very rarely do
I hear anyone asking this question, and it's a great
one. If you can get into long-term alignment with a
customer, you will have them as a customer for a lifetime.

14.   How do you think your boss or board of directors will evaluate the success of this initiative? This one is modified but similar to the question I wrote about above as # 6. Evaluating the success of a new product or service is critical to your customer's success and to yours. Because you are most often meeting with a liaison and not the decision maker, this is an important question to ask. Now, don't be misled by "sales gurus" that tell you to never meet with anybody that's not the decision maker. While I agree that it would be amazing to always meet with the decision maker, very often we have to meet with a liaison. It's a perfectly acceptable part of the total sales process. It's very easy for a sales trainer to tell you never to meet with anyone that's not the decision maker. It's an easy statement to make, but it's much harder to live up to. When you're out on the street selling like we are, you understand exactly what I'm saying. Not everything is a perfect reality.

15.   What do you look for in the companies you do business with? This question is very specific to companies that have an evaluation process as they look to sign up with new vendors. Sometimes there are

credit checks in play. Sometimes you have to be pre-approved. There are all kinds of different variables in the total sales process. So keep in mind, everybody's process is a little bit different.

The questions you ask are mission critical to your success as a sales professional. One of the things that I don't see many companies do is share their success patterns. As it relates to questions, I would highly suggest that your entire company get together and figure out what are the best questions to ask. Don't just get questions from a book like mine. That's great by the way; thank you for buying the book, but you need to evaluate the questions and determine how they advance your sales agenda. Again, it's very important not to ask questions just to ask questions. If all you're doing is filling time in a vacuum, that is a pretty useless way to handle your next sales call. I suggest that you and your team evaluate each and every question with vivid detail. Ask questions for a reason. Don't just ask questions to ask questions. One thing that has really changed since this global pandemic hit is that people have lost patience for almost everything. They lost patience for politics.

They've lost patience for other people's opinions. And they've really lost patience for people that waste their time. Don't be one of those people. Reevaluate all the questions you ask on a sales call, and don't just ask them because you've been asking them for years. Instead, ask yourself these questions ... "Why am I asking this question?" "Will this question advance the conversation further?" "Is this the very best question I could be asking?" "Will this question lead me to a sale?" Oftentimes people will say to me that selling doesn't have to be this hard. Let me tell you this ... selling is very, very difficult. There is no silver bullet. There is no quick fix. It's going to take a lot of hard work for all of us to not only survive but to thrive in a post-pandemic world. And a lot of that will start with the questions that we ask.

***

Chapter Eight: Overcoming the Six Most Common Media Sales Objections

Media salespeople that can effectively handle objections close 40% more business. I would venture to say that any salesperson that can handle objections like a Ninja will sell more. As I have mentioned before, those of you not in the media sales business will need to take my rules from this chapter and apply them to your own sales situation.

Handling objections is a skill that every media salesperson must master. Amidst selling during this global pandemic, objection-handling has taken a little bit of a different twist. Having worked with almost 30,000 salespeople around the globe, I've found that objection-handling is a skill that most salespeople think they have mastered, but that most fail at when put on the spot. Handling objections and not coming across as argumentative or arrogant has a lot to do with being well-practiced. If I've said it once I'll say it a thousand times … professionals practice and amateurs wing it. Who do you want to be? Never forget… planning plus practice equals potential.

At face value, most objections from advertisers are best handled with a success story and not a fact or a statistic, based on my experience. Right now, Brain Swell Media's most recent data suggests that seven out of 10 of our advertisers are buying from an emotional perspective. We have to be very careful about using statistics and data in the sales process. Of course, using data does have its place. But I think you'll see below that when we dissect the six most common media sales objections, there are several ways we can handle them without having to give a fact or a stat. You will see here that I've detailed the six most common objections that I encounter on a daily basis as I'm selling advertising media. You will also notice that these are written out much like a script. Please do not come across to your advertisers as a script-based sales executive, though. Rather, this is set up in such a way that you can practice by yourself—or better yet, with a peer—and get ready to roll.

Objections occur in three scenarios that are easy to replicate and practice around: 1.) When booking meetings. 2.) When you're face-to-face. 3.) When you are virtually hosting a sales call. And with any of these three, preparation is the key to overcoming objections.

Common Media Objection #1:

Advertiser says: "I'm good."

Media Sales Executive: "Good as in?" – (Be silent and listen.)

Advertiser says: "We have enough business."

Media Sales Executive: "Great. Sounds like we need to move you from a new customer marketing plan to a thanking-your-current-customers plan. You do want to thank your current customers, right? Our marketing options cover more than just new customers. We help your customers engage more deeply with you, as well."

Common Media Objection #2:

Advertiser says: "We are cutting back on marketing until the pandemic is over."

Media Sales Executive: "I can certainly understand your concern. When you say, 'pandemic is over,' what does that mean to you?"

Advertiser says: "Well ... over. Dead. Etc."

Media Sales Executive: "My concern is that we are having a moving target date here that is very hard to predict. Advertising does not produce instantaneous results. People need to see your ad many times before they react. Other business owners like you are keeping their names out there so that when the customer is ready to engage, they think of them first. And that is the key—to keep your business top-of-mind."

Common Media Objection #3:

Advertiser says: "I have no budget. It's all spent."

Media Sales Executive: "What about Advertiser A, B, and C?" – (You name three current advertisers.) -

Advertiser says: "What about 'em?"

Media Sales Executive: "I truly feel that your absence is their opportunity! They are all seeing results after a few months of marketing with us. How about I quickly show you some marketing ideas that are working?"

Common Media Objection #4:

Advertiser says: "My Facebook page works well for me."

Media Sales Executive: ""I love to hear that you believe in marketing on social. We love social media, too. The issue is that nearly every business is competing for eyes on Facebook. So, what are you doing to stand out from your competitors?" – (Also, explain that social and digital are different.) Maybe you then explain the Marketing Triangle of Success from Chapter 5.

Common Media Objection #5:

Advertiser says: "No one reads the paper/magazine anymore."

Media Sales Executive: "May I ask you a question? [OK] Whatever your answer is, please don't worry about hurting my feelings. [OK] Do you personally read our newspaper? [NO] It is not surprising at all for me to hear that no one reads the paper when you yourself do not read the paper. It's ok. The survey of one is totally normal. What I can tell you is this ... if we published even one sentence of negativity about you, your feelings would be different about how many people read the paper. Your phone would ring off the hook. Traditional media is not a get-rich-quick plan. It is a tested and proven way to put your name in front of X number of readers every week so that when a customer is ready to buy you are the business they think of first."

Common Media Objection #6:

Advertiser says: "Word of mouth is my best marketing vehicle."

Media Sales Executive: "The problem with WOM is that you lose control of your marketing message. You are asking untrained people to carry your marketing message to the masses. Are you confident they will say what you want them to say about your business?"

Advertiser says: "Yes, I am."

Media Sales Executive: "What if they had a bad experience and did not tell you?"

Advertiser says: "What do you mean?"

Media Sales Executive: "In a word-of-mouth scenario, a bad experience can spiral out of control on social media."

Objection-handling is one of the most critical skill sets that every serious media sales executive should possess. And yet, were you aware that seven in 10 professional sales executives have never taken any type of formal sales training? I guess that's good for me being in the sales training business, but it's a bit scary to think about so many people selling without a formal framework for sales success.

So wherever you fall on the spectrum of training, I encourage you to use these and other scenarios to create some type of flashcard system where you can practice with your peers. I'm not a big fan of role-playing, necessarily, but I do see how practice makes perfect. And serious practice will produce serious results. So I would find a practice partner—someone you trust—and practice these scenarios one-on-one until you are smooth and prepared. It's important because the worst thing you can do is practice when you are on a sales call. Your clients... they deserve better than that.

The formula is pretty straight forward when creating an answer to an objection.

1. Can I reply with a client success story rather than a stat?
2. If I do have a stat as a rebuttal... how can I wrap it into a success story?

3. Often it is not what you say, it is how you say it. So, practice.

4. Empathize, Engage, Inspire. Empathize with the concern. 5. Engage the client with a success story. Inspire them with your confidence.

6. If you do not know the answer, <u>don't make one up.</u>

In the end, be prepared. There are 6-8 objections that are common on your sales calls. Gather them up and create an objection cheat sheet. Planning plus practice equals potential.

***

Chapter Nine: Revamping Sales Decks and Proposals, the New Era of Proposal Creation by the Numbers

This book is really about doing things differently. While there are some elements of my sales process that will probably remain the same until the end of my career, I'm constantly looking for new ways to reinvent and to reinvigorate my total sales game. The COVID global pandemic has forced me to make some fairly significant changes to the way that I present proposals and slide decks. As a point of clarity, a slide deck is the slides a salesperson creates in PowerPoint to show to a customer. A proposal deck normally shows a short review of the capabilities, but primarily focuses on the price of what you are selling.

At this point, I want to back up a step and make this point: Typically, in most sales organizations, there are up to five or six steps to the sales process.

1.   First, you would prospect somebody to get a meeting.

2.   Then you would meet with that customer and conduct a needs assessment to determine their needs, desires, and wants.

3.   Then, you would leave that meeting to go and create a proposal based upon the discovery from the initial meeting.

4.   Then you would once again work hard to set a meeting to present the proposal.

5.   Then you meet again.

6.   Then the customer has to think about things.

7.   Then you have to follow up.

As you can see, this is a moderately long process. Hopefully, one of the things that you have learned reading during this book is that people have lost their patience for just about everything, including the sales process. So when you look through the process as I just explained it, you can see that you actually have seven steps. I would present to you this idea: Let's reduce that to four steps and increase our chances of closing a deal the first time that we have an opportunity to meet with a customer.

In most organizations, the slide deck that the sales team uses is called a capabilities deck. This is the deck that is usually presented live or virtually to a customer at the very first discovery meeting. Because in most sales processes you discover first, then leave the meeting to create a proposal, you are creating a presentation deck and a proposal deck. Two separate tools. I'm going to suggest reducing this process to four steps, where we actually combine the presentation capabilities deck and the proposal deck into one smooth and simultaneous deck. One presentation. Essentially, going to the discovery meeting with ideas and pricing ready to go. Now, I know that this may spit in the face of literally hundreds of years of selling to eliminate so many steps. I have simply found that pandemic fatigued selling will require us to speed up the total sales process. People are emotional and they're impatient. That applies to their personal life and their business life. Now, one thing to note is that I have been doing this combined capabilities and proposal deck together for several years. I have just now learned how effective it has been throughout the COVID-19 sales selling cycle. Who would have ever thought that we would see a global pandemic not only wreck our personal lives, but also our professional lives? Little did I know in creating a shorter sales process that I would actually be doing something prior to the pandemic that would help my teams carry on in a vibrant way throughout the pandemic.

Before we get into the weeds, I think it's important for all of us to recognize that humans are hard-wired to dismiss facts that don't fit into their viewpoints. This is well documented by Adrian Bardon, Ph.D., professor of philosophy at Wake Forest University in Winston-Salem, North Carolina. When we talk about new ideas, I could present a simple fact to you and you could dismiss it as being false--even if there are hard-core facts to back it up. Let me give you an example. Tom Brady spent the first 20 seasons of his career with the New England Patriots, playing in nine Super Bowls and winning six of them—both of those facts being the most of any player in NFL history. Despite this being proven and overly documented in multiple ways by many different people, those that are not fans of Tom Brady would say that we should never look to him for guidance or inspiration. It's as if they're denying the fact that he is a winner. It's as if they're denying the fact that he is a champion. At their core they would realize that the statement I just made is factually accurate. But in the psychology of human behavior, denialism is a person's choice to deny reality as a way to avoid a psychologically uncomfortable truth. This is documented in Professor Bardon's research.

When it comes to making a significant change to your sales life, it's important to recognize that you will need to set aside denialism and focus on rational ways to shorten the sales process and get deals done faster, even if it feels to you like the wrong way to do it. I would not, and have never, suggest that a sales professional do something unethical. I just want you to be thinking about the feeling you have in the pit of your stomach when a sales coach like me tells you to try something new. A lot of times there is this feeling deep down in your stomach that just makes you uneasy. It makes you feel uncomfortable. That is your inner spirit challenging you to ask more questions— challenging you to think through something in a very vibrant way. And there's nothing wrong with that at all. However, I would suggest to you that every time I've achieved significant success it always started with an uneasy feeling. Your brain is trying to tell you, "Warning. Watch out. Something might be coming that could endanger you." It is ok. Because on the other side of things we know, years of experience tell us that very often we experience uncomfortable feelings that come before success. Those feelings happen because we are attempting to risk a change in what we perceive as normal.

That's a lengthy preamble to a very basic philosophy shift in post-COVID selling. However, I felt it was important for me to share that with you because this is one area that can be so dramatically improved in your sales life. Yet, most people simply don't make this change I'm about to suggest next because of the uncomfortable feeling they get in the pit of their stomach. That, or they are suffering from denialism--an irrational action that withholds the validation of a historical experience or event, when a person refuses to accept an empirically verifiable reality. Again, I would encourage you to look into the research of Professor Bardon. What he has to say about the psychology behind change is quite influential. It definitely helped me in my quest to be the very best sales coach I can be.

Before we move on ... let me just be clear on Tom Brady, as well. I am not personally a fan of Mr. Brady's, from a football perspective. The reason is because of my lifelong obsession with sports teams from Chicago. But, I'm able to set aside my team prejudice and recognize a winner. I am able to identify what makes Brady very successful. He is exceptional at identifying repeatable patterns of success. He identifies them, and then figures out ways to repeat the success. Then, he shares that success with others and teaches his team to be successful. And he repeated those patterns of success taking the Buccaneers in Tampa to a Super Bowl® victory. But he doesn't stop there. He also identifies repeatable patterns of failure. Then, unlike so many other people, he creates plans to remove those patterns from his personal life and his football life. And further, to the point of larger success, he shares what he has learned to help other teammates to remove repeatable patterns of failure, too. Sure, most of the time, success will come from his personal abilities and talent. But I have observed that he identifies repeatable things that work and he repeats them. From my perspective it appears to be one of his greatest assets. So how does this apply to sales and proposals?

As a sales training company, my colleagues and I have had the opportunity to study over 1,200 pages of slide decks, presentation decks, capability decks, and proposals. One of the things that we learned in evaluating these materials from various companies of various sizes is that very little was universal. This is a scary thought. What we asked of the companies that presented us capabilities decks and proposals for consideration is that they separate what they sent to us into two separate folders. In one folder we only wanted capabilities decks and slide decks that earned business--those that were either combined or separate that actually earned business and closed deals. Then, we asked them to create a separate folder and put in that folder decks, sales materials, or proposals that did NOT win business. What we wanted to do was figure out what were the similarities of the materials that won business versus the similarities of the materials that did not earn business. What we found will probably not surprise you dramatically. But my hope is that you will take this information to heart and make a big change towards the creation of a combined capabilities and proposal deck. From this research we found some great takeaways that have influenced my coaching, training and public speaking.

One of our biggest takeaways from our research was that the companies that combined their capabilities deck with a pricing proposal almost always closed more deals than those that had this piece of the sales process in two separate steps. The teams that combined the two of them together to create a less than ten-page combined slide deck, closed about 40% more deals than those with separate decks and steps in their processes. When the submitting sales teams that offered a combined deck were asked how they could present ideas without meeting the client, they shared that they did this by making assumptions based on past business with other companies that were very similar. Now, at this point some of you might be saying we have too much to sell and there's no way to combine this into one step or one single deck. I would challenge you that I work with companies large and small all around the globe and this same objection comes up every single time I suggest this. As a matter of fact, in some cases it's very much like a knock-down-drag-out fight. It doesn't have to be that way. No matter how you feel about something, try not to deny the facts when someone presents them to you.

The next big takeaway from our research was to understand that the phrase "it sure would be nice if" can kill your sales life, your sales decks, and your proposals. Working from this mentality, a great number of sales professionals will tweak every single proposal to meet their specific needs. They tweak every individual capabilities deck to meet their individual needs. Or, if it's not their needs, it's their personal taste. This can be very time-consuming and can also be pretty darn dangerous. Most successful sales teams that I work with have a very universal approach to capabilities decks and proposal presentation. There is very little customization to the sales decks. Allowing sales reps to tweak on decks allows them to introduce their prejudice, taste, or preconceived notions into a proven sales process.

Another big takeaway was that 79% of our test users always scanned any new page they came across and only 18% actually read what we put on the paper, word by word. Another 3% did not read at all. They just looked at the pictures. In doing some research I found a company called Hyler-Hillman that came up with an almost identical result in its case studies.

The next compelling insight we found was that of the combined decks that earned business, 65% offered three pricing options to the customer. As it relates to the pricing options, the next thing we observed is that when they offered three pricing options, option number one was always presented as the most expensive—maybe a figure that would require the client to stretch their budget a bit. We also observed that the average page count was ten total pages/slides or less in the deck. And we noticed that a number of additional pages were put in place to explain things that most normal humans wouldn't understand anyway—like technical specs or company history.

In addition, we observed that 45% of the proposals that won business had 50% less text than those that did not earn business. There was a lot less text on specs, deadlines, options, ideas, and other related information. The text was replaced with more pictures and graphic examples of what the salesperson was trying to get across.

Another finding of importance, of the proposals and slide decks that earned business, 55% featured testimonials or case studies. One of the things I do in nearly all of my presentations is to front load the conversation with success stories. I often equate it to priming a water pump. Growing up on an Iowa farm, it was not uncommon for us to have to pump water or fluids from one tank to another. To get the process going you would have to prime the pump. Meaning, you would have to fill the pump with water to get the water flowing from one tank to another. The pump was not self-priming nor was it strong enough to move the water without a little bit of help on the front end. Similarly, priming a conversation with success stories forces the customer to be thinking about success--the success we've created for others.

One of the things I find very helpful is including testimonials in the slide deck and then including a photograph alongside the testimonial. I don't ask my customers to write testimonials for me. Rather, I write testimonials for them to approve. Then I go on LinkedIn and find their photograph and include that in the slide deck. A testimony without a photo is sort of like a cinnamon roll without the frosting. It's okay, but it's not great.

The final area of learning was that nearly all of the combined slide decks that won business did NOT feature slides about company history. One of the things that I observed is that the most skipped-over piece of any slide deck is a company's history. Our company history is of no importance to the customer and they really, quite honestly, don't care. But this is one of those battles that I'm not willing to fight about. No matter how many facts I present to you, that nobody cares about your company history, every CEO or COO or VP of sales insists on including company history in every slide deck. I've actually observed, in watching webcams, potential customers roll their eyes as the salesperson walks through the history of the company. Think about this friends, and this is the last thing I'll say about it, they took a meeting with you so they probably know a bit about you and have re-searched you online. Company history is something that has been in presentations since the good old days of Glengarry Glen Ross. But realize this: Nobody cares about your company history. If they did they would have researched you in advance. I promise.

Now, let's talk about the slide decks and proposals that lost business. One of the biggest observations was that slide decks over 10 pages consistently closed far less deals than those under 10 pages. There was a sweet spot at seven pages that seemed to work much better. Yet, nearly every proposal in the lost business pile is more than 10 pages.

In the proposals that lost business, only 30% had three pricing options. The vast majority either did not have pricing or only included one pricing option.

Clearly, when it comes to price, customers like choices. Don't try to tell me, it just depends on what you're selling. That phrase, "it just depends," very of-ten cripples sale professionals. As I stated before in this book, don't live by the exception. Rather, live by the rule.

We further learned in these proposals and decks that lost business that over 50% included details on specs, deadlines, and other super detailed information that could have simply been presented after the sale is closed. Remember, from my previous points on personality traits in chapter four, you want to create the best slide deck for each personality type. Most of the time there's just one slide deck that is created to be used by everyone. Or, there is one master deck that all the reps can customize. Customization kills, from what we have learned from Tom Brady and our research. If salespeople keep doing things the way they like, individually, they miss out on the ability to leverage successful repeatable patterns of success.

One of the overwhelming pieces of data that our team found, in addition to these other findings, is that proposals that lost business contained fewer pictures and were overwhelmingly text-heavy. Also, 45% did not feature testimonials or case studies of any kind.

To recap, the big universal takeaways from both "won" and "lost" business proposals are as follows:

1.   Combining the capabilities and proposal into one deck works.

2.   Ten pages or less per deck.

3.   Present testimonials and case studies up front in the deck.

4.   Provide three pricing options.

5.   Remove as much text as you can and replace it with pictures.

6.   Highlighted keywords tend to draw in the user's eye.

7.   Bulleted lists, rather than paragraphs, tend to be read more often.

8.   Those proposals that presented one idea per paragraph were viewed more frequently than those with multiple ideas inside of one paragraph.

9.   Half of the word count can be removed from nearly every proposal, and it will still be very successful.

10.   We observed that in almost every proposal there were a lot of spec and data details that truly

could wait until after the sale. The reason they were included is because there was this one time that this one client asked this one question of this one sales-person and so it was left in there.

11.   Slide decks in proposals should not replicate a conversation.

12.   Remove company history slides.

13.   Leave super technical detail for post sales conversations, unless those details are mission criti-cal to closing the deal.

We can spend an entire day-long workshop on pro-posal, capability, or sales deck creation. My hope is that as salespeople read this chapter, they will recog-nize that they can shorten the process. With a little bit of research, and by making some good assump-tions/recommendations, we should be able to go to any sales meeting with our capabilities and our pric-ing in one continuous simple slide deck that's less than 10 pages. For those who may still might be say-ing, "How can I present ideas to somebody when I have no idea what they want?" I would simply say, make an assumption and give it your best shot. If you're on the sales call and what you thought or assumed is wrong, then don't present the pricing options, just wait on that. If your company has 75 things to sell to one individual, I highly recommend that you do not offer them a buffet of options. If a buffet were the way to go, every restaurant would offer that. They don't. As a point of note, most Michelin starred restaurants offer a menu with less than seven options. Do some research, look at the competitors of the company you're presenting to, and make some realistic and educated guesses as to what that customer is probably going to need. Then, make recommendations to the client. Then, if you know your slide deck inside and out, you can create your live narrative based on what you're hearing in real time. This is just another one of the reasons not to put too much text in your slide decks.

One final thought on presenting slide decks, which we will cover more in the next chapter, is that you want to be prepared to go off-script. There's nothing worse than a salesperson that forces a customer to sit through 25 slides in a one particular order. To be successful in the sales business you're going to have to be able to ad-lib very quickly, honestly, and ethically. If you can make YOUR presentation THEIR presentation, you have a winning scenario on your hands. Don't be a person that is plagued by denialism. The information shared in this chapter is based upon facts, research, and sales presentations I make every day to my customers. I have over 4000 companies that are now selling this way. Over 30,000 reps have been trained to sell this way. They are very successful. Many of them have said to me, "Why have we not been doing this for years?"

***

Chapter Ten: Hosting Virtual Sales Calls that Close Deals

Buyers have been trained during COVID that they don't have to meet with salespeople face to face. Of course, I'd love to meet with them face to face, I prefer face-to-face selling, but when you can't, you've got to get really, really great at selling virtually.

I have ten ideas to share with you, but first, two overall observations: I've noticed over the course of time that I close many more deals with slide decks that are 10 pages or less. I close way more deals with slide decks that feature a lot of testimonials, and a number of case studies. I've also noticed that I personally tend to buy a good deal more from salespeople that know how to present virtually. It's just easier for me to schedule those meetings in a virtual environment than to make time to meet with somebody face to face.

Let me reiterate, I love face-to-face meetings. But what we've learned during COVID is that people understand they don't have to meet with us face to face to get a deal done. Stop forcing something that doesn't need to be forced. Present to the customer in the way that they want to be presented to. Selling virtually has become a common form of selling—one that's very acceptable to all of our prospects, period.

If we feel like once COVID is gone we'll go back to face-to-face selling, we may be setting ourselves up for failure. As of this writing, the Omicron variant is raging across the world. Sure, some things will come back into play. But if COVID has proven anything, it is that dear old Grandma can get on a Zoom® call easily.

What I've observed is that most people think they're great at selling in a virtual world and, quite honestly, they really are not! If you think you are good, read on. Here are 10 ways to sell like a remote sales superstar. The first idea I'll share with you is the understanding that how you present yourself really does matter. I hear from a lot of people that they feel like how they look online and how they present online doesn't necessarily matter to anybody except their boss, and this is just not true.

You can really tell a dramatic difference between a professional and someone that's a little bit newer to selling based on their presentation style. This is not a Millennial versus Boomer conversation. This is a conversation about professional selling strategies. Presenting live in front of somebody is very different than presenting to someone virtually because there are so many different pieces of the body language puzzle that are missing or different.

When we look at how many people are visual learners, you'll see that approximately 65% of people learn by seeing things. Only about 35% of people actually learn by reading. The vast majority of people are visual. So the first point to take away from this chapter is that if you're selling with the phone only, you're missing out on a vital part of the total sales process. I'm not suggesting that virtual selling replaces face-to-face selling. I'm not suggesting that virtual is the only way to go. I'm not suggesting that face to face is the only way to go. I'm suggesting that most buyers today have come to understand and accept that they don't have to meet with us face to face to get something done. We all know that this is accurate and it's true. Now, would I rather be in front of somebody face to face? The answer is absolutely. But when I can't meet them face to face, the next best thing is for me to present to them through some type of virtual meeting setup, whether it's Zoom® or GoToMeeting® or Microsoft Teams®. Whatever setup we choose, if we recognize that 65% of people are visual learners, then we'd better pay attention—and we'd better be using all the technology we have at our disposal.

So, you may ask, what about the other 5% of people? Those 5% learn by experiencing something. They don't learn by seeing it. They can't learn by listening. They learn by experiencing something. Thank goodness this only represents about 5% of people. But what do we do with those folks in a virtual selling world? It is a lot about sharing success stories and case studies. We need to pivot quickly and just move to testimonials and success-based visuals, such as pictures of a happy client with a small bit of text that shows why they love us.

No matter how a potential customer learns, buying executives at B2B and B2C companies ranked trust ahead of low price and superior innovation. Most salespeople feel like trust can only be built in a face-to-face sales world, and that's simply not accurate. If you were to take the five letters of trust and break them down individually, T-R-U-S-T, we will see that if we approach trust with a sales strategy, we can win in the virtual sales world, too.

I find that this word "trust" can be broken down into an acronym, where the letter T stands for "transparency," the letter R for "relevance," the letter U for "understanding," the letter S for "strategy," and the last letter T for "track record." Building trust is paramount to your success in any endeavor-- especially the sales business. So what can we do in a virtual sales world to present in a more trust-based way?

Let's take a look at the letter T ...for transparency. That's transparency in pricing. That's transparency in the way we present our offerings. It would be transparency in the questions that we ask, and how we answer the customer's questions, being really an open book. If at any point in time you come across as being a "salesperson," then I think you've got a problem on your hands.

The letter R in the word trust stands for relevance. It's being relevant in presenting solutions and ideas to somebody that are truly relevant to their needs. The only way you would know this is by doing significant research in advance of the conversation, or by asking some really great questions. In chapter five, we talked about the questions to ask and the questions not to ask. Relevance is all about you proving to a customer or potential customer that you know their pain points. Asking questions can determine those pain points, but coming to a conversation and asking a question like, "Tell me more about your business" is a surefire way to not advance the ball down the field, period. Questions like that lead your prospect to think that you've not prepared for the meeting. Relevance is me saying things like, "In preparation for our meeting I did some research on your company and discovered A-B and C ... are these areas still a priority to you?"

The U in the word trust stands for understanding. Understanding is your ability to be able to link the needs and desires and wants of that potential customer into a congruent thought that will reference their pain points and how what you're selling will solve or eliminate those pain points. Note that understanding is different from making assumptions. Assumptions are guesses that you'll make towards an end goal.

Understanding is asking questions and presenting ideas and working with that person as a partner to potentially close the deal. The more you understand their problem, typically the more your solution can solve their problem. We've got to be careful here, though, because a lot of times people feel like the only way you can understand somebody is to ask a ton of questions. And that leads to a poor customer needs assessment, and a poor customer needs experience. If this does not make sense to you, refer back to chapter four.

The S in trust stands for strategy. Strategy is really about you recommending solutions to the customer that will alleviate their pain points or solve-their-problems strategy. It is a lot about you making recommendations. You're supposed to be the advisor at the meeting. If they were an expert at what it is you were selling, they probably wouldn't have taken the meeting with you. Never forget that 44% of buyers find their solutions with no help from a salesperson. So you've got to really focus in on what strategy means to the person that you're meeting with. Do they need help saving money? Do they need help saving time? Do they need help making money? Strategy is about you presenting and putting your best foot forward with ideas.

One of the worst things that I see people do is not come to a meeting with ideas. But, you may ask, how do I bring an idea if I do not know what they want? Guess! Make some strategic assumptions. If you get to the meeting and your ideas are way off point, do not present them. You need to come to every meeting with ideas ready to go that are based on relevant things that you know about that company that you've found in your research or in working with their competition. Conveying strategic ideas is simply critical. Keep in mind, however, that strategy is oftentimes not something the customer is focused on; they're more focused on tactics and not big strategy. It's important for us to be able to work with them carefully, as relates to this, so that we are delivering strategic ideas and not just fulfilling their wants and desires. Very often their wants and desires are not going to lead them to the ultimate goal even if they define a goal and you fulfill their current wants, you still might not be giving them exactly what it is that they need. Thus, you're going to have a customer that will be happy for a shorter period of time. And that's not what we're going for.

The last T in trust stands for track record. This is your ability to prove to somebody that you have a track record of success with other clients like them--that you are seasoned at solving their problems. That they are not the first person to try your product or service. Now, if you're in a situation where you're a startup and you have no track record, then that is a completely different conversation for a different day. In this particular circumstance, I'm going to assume that you do have some customers that are happy. I am going to assume you're able and ready to relay those satisfied customer stories to the person that you're meeting with on the virtual sales call.

When hosting a call with somebody, a new client perhaps, I like to make sure that I front load the conversation with success stories. It's called "priming the conversation." This allows someone's brain to be focused on success and the fact that you provide success. Do you recall what priming is? Previous chapter. Priming the pump. At least remove obstacles and problems that are typically in their way. How you present yourself when selling virtually, if you think about breaking down the word T.R.U.S.T. as we did here, will almost always be stronger if you're clear in your mind on how to handle the circumstance and scenario. Simply put, how you present yourself is mission critical in a virtual world.

The second idea I want to share with you for when you're presenting virtually is to make sure that you're creating a virtual environment that is actually ideal for somebody to absorb your data and your information. You need to eliminate background noise and distractions. All too often people that are hosting meetings don't take into account that the person on the other side of the video screen or the phone call or whatever, is trying to pay attention to you, but if there's background noise and distractions, maybe you're not even hearing them because you're wearing a headset. This may be the case if you wear a two-eared headset that blocks out the noise around you; the person on the other end of the line can hear all the background noise in high fidelity. Not only can they hear that noise through the phone, but they can also see that noise and the distractions on your video camera. Let me give you an example. Let's say that you happen to be working one day from Starbucks and you're making sales calls. That seems all fine and dandy because the coffee is always better when it's made for you at the store. Right? Well, the problem is that the background noise may not seem like a big deal to you, but unless you're using the right kind of microphone, the background noise is going to be overwhelming and quite a distraction for the person on the other end. If you are thinking that this really doesn't matter and that people just need to get over it, that's not true. It is your responsibility to create the perfect virtual meeting environment. What you do and how you present yourself are critical to closing deals. The best product in the world, presented in a poor way, can be outsold by an inferior product with a polished sales team. Eliminating background noise and distractions shows that you're professional, and that this wasn't just an off-the-cuff meeting. Prove that you actually prepared for the meeting and that it's important to you.

Now for number three: how you sound is mission critical too. There are two different ways that you can better sell yourself, because half of the battle is selling yourself, so that the prospect or customer will actually trust you. A lot of times you'll see people on the cable news channels using their Apple AirPods in a meeting as both a microphone and as a way to hear. This is not how professionals present themselves. The audio fidelity is fine for listening to music and talking to your pals, but it's not good enough for a high level professional virtual meeting. They are far better than using your internal computer mic, but they are far from delivering superior audio fidelity.

When you think about how people learn, we mentioned before that 65% are visual learners and 37% are auditory learners. That means seeing and listening are critical to someone's acceptance and interpretation of what it is that you're saying and doing. This is why I highly recommend to everyone who conducts professional virtual meetings, invest in a nice headset or some quality type of microphone.

The reason that I choose to use a microphone and not a headset is just because of the way it looks. I prefer the clean look of not having a big old headset on my head with a microphone in front of my face. However, I would rather see someone with a big old headset on with a good microphone than not be able to understand someone clearly, because they're wearing their ear buds rather than using a quality microphone.

Now, if you choose to use a headset, there are three or four different companies that make exceptional options with wonderful fidelity. If you're going to buy a headset, make sure you buy one that covers both of your ears to eliminate distractions and background noise. There are some very good companies out there, Jabra, Blue Parrot, and Plantronics, that all offer great headsets in a price range from $65 to $150. If you're deciding to use an actual microphone like a podcast microphone, I would not get one that is Bluetooth-connected. Rather, I would get one that actually has a USB cord. The reason for this is to eliminate technical issues. There are several great microphones out there that are affordable. One of the most popular is the Blue microphone called a Snowball mic that you can buy from Amazon or other retailers for as little as $65.

To sum up, invest in yourself and buy a quality mic and/or headset. If you choose to buy a mic, get a pair of wired earbuds, too. Do not rely on your computer's mic and speakers, even in a virtual sales meeting world.

Remember, when you say to one of your prospects, "Does this sound okay," they will more than likely say yes. The reason they're doing that is because they're being polite, even if it doesn't sound good. They're still going to say yes. If you're going to take yourself seriously, you need to get serious sales tools. Sort of like playing the game of golf. You could get away with a cheap set of clubs, but unless you're pretty good, those cheap set of clubs are only going to get you so far. If you're really going to take your golf game to the next level, you need some training, some practice, and a nice set of golf clubs that are custom fit for you.

Once the audio is squared away the next thing you need to do is make sure that you look good. That leads us to idea number four of this chapter, looking good on your webcam.

One of the problems I observe when I'm looking at somebody's webcam is that they're oftentimes trying to sit in front of a window, which makes them backlit. When somebody is backlit, it makes them look like they're a part of the witness protection program, and all you see is a silhouette. Yes, this does matter! I would highly encourage you to purchase a small soft light box from Amazon or an online photography retailer to make your webcam setup look great. Selens Photography Table Top Lighting kit Portable Softbox Led Lamp offers continuous soft light for your face. The next thing you want to do is make sure that your webcam is actually level with your eyes. A lot of times you'll notice that you can see people's ceiling fans in the background of their webcam. The reason for this is because the laptop is lower than their head, and so they have to tip the laptop back. This is also a very unflattering look up your nostrils. You want to make sure that your webcam, using some type of leveling device like the TRUNIUM Adjustable Ergonomic Aluminum Laptop Holder Stand for Desk, is at the same height as your eyes. You're going to be looking directly into the webcam, and positioning yourself in front of a blank wall or a nice bookcase is excellent. Another important tip: be careful with the things that are in the background. Because if you happen to have anything in the background that is of a political or religious nature, you may want to move that to avoid any type of conflicts. I actually recorded a video on YouTube called "How not to be a webcam zombie," and that might be a great reference, as well. Remember, how you present yourself is mission critical in building trust--and trust is important.

When selling virtually. I also make sure to really watch my clients' faces for clues. Now, not every time does my customer share their webcam. But, I want to make sure that I share mine. The reason for this is that so much is lost when you can't see someone. Invite them to share their webcam. If they don't want to engage, it's not a big deal. Definitely don't force someone to share their webcam. What I've found is that most of the time people do. And I want to watch their faces very, very carefully to make sure that they're paying attention and following along. Coming up, I'll give you a few more tips on the pacing of the virtual presentation.

What makes it really easy to see if somebody is paying attention is if they're wearing eyeglasses. With those that wear eyeglasses, typically you can see what they're looking at in the lens of their glasses, as they stare back. More than anything, don't get so wrapped up in your presentation that you aren't watching your customer's face for clues. I want to see if they're surprised. If they're angry. If they're fearful. If they're disgusted. If they're happy. If they're showing a face of contempt. Whatever the circumstances, it's important just like if you're in front of that person to really focus in on what their facial expressions are adding to the conversation. Then, I don't want to say something like, "Hey, Bill, I see your nose is all wrinkled. Are you upset with me about that point or do you have a question?" That is a bit too obvious. Instead of referencing the customer, I simply register the fact that they look like they're not happy, and I say something along the lines of, "Perhaps you have a different way of thinking about this?" Or, "Maybe there is something you'd like me to further clarify? I'm happy to do that." In the end, watching the customer's face when the webcam is turned on separates amateur salespeople from professional salespeople.

The next idea in this chapter is number six. And this is to understand that you want to unshare your screen often. When you're asking questions, be sure that your screen share is off. You want to re-engage with the prospect often. It is mission critical. Un-sharing your screen allows your webcam to come full screen, and their webcam to come full screen. I'm unsharing the screen at the end of each slide or every two slides. The reason I'm doing this is to gain under-standing from the customer that I'm selling to. When I unshare my screen I'm not going to ask a question like, "Do you have any questions?" Or, "What ques-tions do you have so far?" Instead, I'm going to ask better questions than that.

Here are some examples:

1.   What else can I share with you about that par-ticular point?

2.   How could I explain this better?

3. How is my speed in presenting this? Do you like it? Am I going too fast? Am I going too slow?

4. Am I covering what you want covered?

5. Am I headed in the right direction?

6. Do you want me to dig deeper on that?

7. Any question, no matter how small, is welcome. I love questions, please. Any questions, ask away.

Those are some sample questions, and you may have some others. But consider un-sharing your screen at the end of each slide to ask for clarification. I have been on literally hundreds of virtual sales calls, and once that screen share goes live, you are reduced to a 1x1 version of yourself. Think about that for a second. That's not smart.

So remember, the questions you ask will often lead the conversation in the direction that you want it to go. In addition, make sure that you use silence to your advantage. We'll talk about this concept several times in this book. Silence allows someone to comprehend, absorb, and think. It's called, giving the customer time to soak. Soak time is just like what it implies, like a sponge. It gives them an opportunity to soak up what you're saying, digest it, and then move on. As a matter of fact, in some presentations I'll even say, "Let me give you a couple of seconds to think about that. And then I'll move on to my next point."

Then I'll pause, wait maybe five to six seconds, and then say to them, "What do you think? Ready to move on, or do you have other questions for me?"

Idea number seven of 10 is to understand how to use your virtual pen to engage more deeply. The virtual pen is the pen tool that's built into any screen-sharing system that allows you to draw on the screen. When I say things like, "Please look at your screen. I'm going to draw," I always notice that people look up from whatever it is they're doing.

The reason that I bring this up is because you have to actively reengage the customer in a virtual meeting. Very often, in most virtual meetings, you will find that people tend to drift. They tend to daydream. They tend to go other places than where you are. Engaging people is part and parcel to your success in hosting a virtual meeting. So I actually like to set up some of my slides to make sure there's white space for me to write on. For example, there's a particular slide that I often use called the consumer buying cycle. It's a flowchart that shows the path that a buyer will take before they buy a particular product or service from a company. I use my pen to circle things, highlight things, and draw lines. An engaged customer is paying attention. When they pay attention it helps you and it helps them. Because I do a lot of work in the technology space, I oftentimes have to draw things on maps, or I'll have to do little diagrams. So I always like to make sure within my presentation that I have several pages that are blank, that I can potentially draw on using the virtual pen. Again, this encourages deeper engagement and deeper understanding. It also allows you to make the meeting seem less like a presentation, and a lot more like a show and tell. Sort of like, "Hey, let me show you this. Let me show you what that would look like."

Idea number eight of 10 in selling virtually like a superstar is to recognize that you need to train your family, your pets, and everybody else that when you're hosting a meeting it's just as if that person is sitting in the same room. What I've noticed oftentimes is that during the COVID selling era, people think it's cute to have their cat in their lap or their dog in the background or things that are funny on the wall behind them. There are certain circumstances where this could be appropriate. But by now you should be able to have your family and your cat trained to not be on the screen when you're hosting a meeting. The number of people that have told me that this type of behavior makes them crazy is staggering. In one call, there was a cat and a parrot on the rep's webcam. It was cute for three minutes, and then it became super annoying. And, it is not because I am 49. It is because they were asking me to buy $15k in software. This is a serious decision. This isn't a generational thing. This is a respect thing. Meaning that when you're hosting a meeting with somebody, it should be in a professional way and not in a comical way. While there is some certain latitude for kids that might be at home from school or things like that, by the time you read this book we should have all figured out this work-from-home thing, though. Even when you're back in the office, you're probably going to do more virtual sales presentations than ever before because during COVID prospects were trained that they don't have to meet with you face to face. They have accepted virtual as a suitable replacement.

Idea number nine: Prepare to go off-script. The reason this is important is because, as we all know, very, very often a prospect will take us down a side road and have a discussion, and we wonder to ourselves how in the world did we ever get here? There are a couple of ways to handle this. One is to go where they want to go. Ask, "Is this the direction you wanted me to take the presentation? Are the ideas that I'm sharing in alignment with what you envisioned when you took this meeting?" Most of the time when things go off the tracks, salespeople aren't prepared for it. And so they tend to get a little bit frustrated. Don't get frustrated. Know your slide deck inside and out. Don't prepare it five seconds before you call somebody. Just recognize that you're going to probably need to go off script and don't be afraid to jump around. There's nothing worse than a salesperson that forces a customer to sit through every single slide in their deck. Be prepared to jump around. Let the client know that it's okay if they want to jump around--this meeting is all about them.

Let me restate this. There's truly nothing worse than a sales rep that is being forced to follow an exact slide deck in sequential order. Think about this from the perspective of the listener. And if you happen to have a multitude of slides, be sure not to put slide numbers in the bottom corner. Once you get over about 12 slides, most people are thinking to themselves, when will this sermon be over?

Idea number 10 is that practice makes perfect. This one is easy to say, but it's much harder to execute. I am not talking about role-playing. I'm talking about not being an amateur. I tell people all the time, amateurs wing it and professionals practice. It might be wise to have the meeting in advance and record it in the virtual environment. That way, you can practice every aspect of the meeting and make sure you know all of the technology inside and out. And for goodness sake, please arrive early to your virtual meetings. There's nothing worse than a salesperson that shows up at a meeting late and the client has been sitting online ... waiting for them.

If for some reason you're reading this book today and you truly think that once a vaccine is stuck in everybody's arm that we're going to go back to sales as usual, I would say that you're just crazy. And, I am not making a political statement by saying that. Again, just to be clear, I love face-to-face meetings. But what we've learned in COVID is that people understand they don't have to meet with us face to face to get a deal done. Stop forcing something that doesn't need to be forced. Present to the customer in the way that they want to be presented. Selling virtually has become a common form of selling that is very acceptable to all of our prospects, period. Now, just get better at hosting virtual meetings will ya?

***

Chapter Eleven: A New Way to Ask for the Sale

In this chapter, new techniques to close the sale without acting like a salesperson.

There are usually two points during every sales call that are mildly awkward. Most salespeople will say that those two are the beginning and the end of every scheduled sales call with a prospective client, since both of these can present a unique set of challenges. At the beginning of the sales call, we're trying to figure out how to quickly connect to build rapport with the customer. And at the end of the sales call, we have to get the client to let loose of their purse strings and give us some money.

Even the most seasoned sales pro will tell you that without a plan and without practice, these two awkward areas can trip up a sales professional for years. So let's dig deep into this issue and figure out a way to make a positive change in our sales lives. Let's create a repeatable pattern of success. Shall we?

If you have ever spoken to a long-distance runner, they will tell you that the way you begin the race sets a precedent for the way you will probably end it. For instance, if you start the race too fast, you may not have enough energy to win in the end. And if you save all your gas to the end of the race, you may be too far behind the pacesetter to close the gap and win.

Now, I think we can all agree, there is way more to running a marathon than just the beginning and the end of the race. But this analogy gives us a scenario that we can potentially use as an example to build upon as we explore our client meetings. One takeaway from the marathon runner example is that if we want to end the race strong, we have to start the race smart.

Here's another example. Let's look at great storytelling for a minute. We know that every great story needs three components: a beginning, a middle, and an end. You need to start the story strongly by giving the reader a compelling reason why they should keep reading. Then, as a reader, if you get to the end of the book and it doesn't conclude in a way that's dramatic, you will often feel like you've wasted time reading the book. A lackluster ending can really let you down. Just as with the racing example, there's a lot more in those pages between the beginning and the end, but you can see that there's a similarity between the two.

As a media sales and marketing professional for over 30 years, I think both of these are great examples of what we need to do to create a plan to make sure we start our sales calls strong and end them strong. We shouldn't be lopsided at all in this attempt. We should be well-practiced, and we should understand that if we start strong, we will probably finish strong, as well.

So let's look at how we sales pros can set ourselves up for success in the media sales business and host the very best meetings to help us achieve our goals. First, I suggest that we start with the end.

What is the one thing that nearly every sales manager asks us to do on a regular basis? Ask for the order, right? Yet, asking for the order can be one of the most awkward situations, even for veteran salespeople. Why? Because it's that point in every conversation where we have to move into "sales mode." Or do we? I don't see the end of the sales calls where you ask for the order as a "yes" or "no" type of question or situation. Sometimes, I can tell that a potential buyer is ready to go, and it's very easy to move them on to the next step. In my experience, though, the majority of the time they're holding back some of their cards and I truly don't know exactly what it is they're thinking. Even in the middle of the sales call when I ask some really great questions, I don't always know exactly what they're thinking. I need a little more engagement. So at the end of the sales call, if I ask a yes-or-no question, I will probably hear a "Well, let me think about it" response. I suppose that is better than a "no." But is it, really? Are potential clients telling you that they need to think about it as a way to end the sales call? Or do they really need to think about it? Or, are they just not telling you "no" because you are a nice person? Or do they just hate saying no? Or are they afraid that if they say no that you will go into a desperate sales rant to save the deal? All of these questions are valid. And these questions have led me to a unique closing technique that I call the 1-to-10 close.

The 1-to-10 close is an easy way to ask for the order and to engage more deeply with the client. It sounds something like this ... "Bonnie, thanks so much for the opportunity to meet with you today. I think this has been a really great conversation. If you don't mind me asking, on a scale of 1 to 10, 1 meaning you're really not that interested, and 10 meaning you're ready to write me a check today, where are you at?"

This 1-to-10 closing technique allows me to re-engage more deeply with the customer and really see where they're at in their mind, related to buying. If a client says to me they are a 5, I simply ask them what I need to do or say or what questions I can answer to get them to be more like a 6 or 7. If someone says they are a 5, that tells me that they are about at the 50/50 mark as to whether they should buy or not. If I don't engage more deeply, I only have a 50% chance of closing the deal. If I had not used the 1-to-10 technique, I would bet that they would have said they wanted to think about it, and I would not have had a chance to give them more decision-making details. If a client were to say to me that they are at 3, I would simply ask them what I can do or say or what questions I can answer that might get them to be closer to a 5 or a 6. Thus, I have just attempted to move them from a "no" to at least a 50/50 shot.

I truly believe that if a customer is at 3, they will never tell you unless you ask them for deeper engagement. If they are at a 3 and they are bold enough to say "no," they fully expect you to jump back at them and get aggressive and try to close them. Who likes that? When you continue to sell after a "no," you are setting yourself up for future failure. Because you have just solidified in their minds that you are a typical sales-person—pushy, over the top, and money-hungry to close a deal. What is interesting to me is the number of times when I press for more during the closing pro-cess, only to realize that the client just does not want to say no to me, because I am a darn nice guy, or they just don't want to hurt my feelings. So again, the 1-to-10 closing technique, when paired with a solid sales call opener, can create a strong strategy for closing success.

Now, let's talk about the start of the sales call for just a minute. I do not like to start with bologna. I like to start strong. So I first validate time. "Thanks, Bonnie, for the 20 minutes today. Do you still have 20 minutes?" Then, I set my three-point agenda and make sure that they agree with the agenda. And then I begin sharing my success stories. Because let me emphasize, I truly believe that starting the call with bologna forces you to engage in making a bologna sandwich. And I simply don't have time for that. Do you?

Being great in sales is all about creating repeatable patterns of success. What is your prospecting process and how do you repeat success? What are the five main questions you ask on every sales call that you know will work? What are the stories you share that almost always get you a positive response? How will you end your next sales call to get past the "I need to think about it"? In today's emotional sales environment, you cannot do what you have always done. What you did in the past may not get you to where you need to be in the future. Growing in sales is about adjusting. So, the real question is this ... are you willing to adjust to close more deals? The 1-10 close... what do you think? Just like you, I want to ask for the sale and get a yes from the client. But, let me ask you this... would you rather have a no from the client or be ghosted? So much of our time is wasted in not getting the no. The 1-10 close allows you to get to the true answer faster in a way that engages and gets you more data to work with as you attempt to seal the deal.

***

Chapter Twelve: Stop Being Ghosted by Clients After a Sales Call

Here are six ways to stop clients from simply disappearing after a sales call.

Ghosting is a relatively new colloquialism that refers to the act of abruptly cutting off contact with someone, without giving that person any warning or explanation for doing so. Even when the person being ghosted reaches out to reinitiate contact or gain closure, they're met with silence.

Out here in sales land this phenomenon happens to all of us and, unfortunately, often at a higher frequency than we would like to admit.

Has this happened to you? You had a great meeting with a potential client and they've asked you for a proposal. You go back to the office and you are excited. You create the proposal. You send over the requested proposal with the anticipation of hearing back soon. Then, everything goes dark. You hear nothing. Every day you play a game of what feels like hide and seek. You reach out by email or phone. You hear nothing. In some cases, you begin to stalk the advertiser by driving past their business. You hear nothing. At a certain point, you become frustrated with yourself. You think maybe you did something wrong. Well, maybe you did.

Ghosting is not necessarily a new phenomenon for salespeople, it's just that now the behavior has an actual name associated with it. And since it's really nothing new for a salesperson to experience, why are we surprised when it happens yet again?

But it doesn't have to be like this, generally speaking. So let's look at six ways to avoid being ghosted by an client/advertiser.

STRATEGY #1: Acknowledge the ghost. At the beginning and end of every sales call with a client, I'm vividly clear about the expectations for the meeting and the expectations for the follow-up. Because typically, there are two awkward moments in every sales call. The beginning. And the end. So, why not just talk about it upfront?

For example, I might say, "Thank you so much for the time today, Bob. At the end of our conversation today

I would love to set up a clear plan for follow-up. If your answer is yes … wonderful. If your answer is no … that's okay, we can always work together at some point in the future. Or, if your answer is that you need to think about it … that's no problem. We'll set a very clear plan for following up together. A plan that meets your exact needs and decision-making timeline."

When you begin sales calls by setting yourself up for success, you normally end the sales call with success. If you begin the sales call with a bunch of the normal bologna that accompanies the typical rapport-building, then you are destined to end the call with an equal amount of bologna.

STRATEGY #2: You must own the follow-up process or you will lose the deal. Very often salespeople will give control of the follow-up over to the cllient. And very often the client will say they will call you back. We all know this is a flat-out lie, in most cases. So, why do we allow the client to control the follow-up? Because we don't know what else to do. But know this: there should always be a plan in place to control the follow-up with the client.

Very often I will end the sales call by getting out my phone or looking at my calendar and creating a meeting invite for the follow-up. When I create that follow-up I create a short, 10-minute meeting on the calendar. That way when the follow-up meeting appears on the client's calendar, it looks like a very short meeting and is less likely to be canceled.

STRATEGY #3: Agree on the best plan for follow-up. A lot of times when you end the sales call, there is not a clear plan nor an agreed-upon plan. Take ownership of the follow-up and be sure that both parties agree that the follow-up plan is crystal clear. You might even ask some questions like, "What is the best way for me to follow up with you? Do you prefer texts? Smoke signals? Carrier pigeon? Or email?"

Now, all kidding aside, my follow-up preference would be by phone. But if you happen to be selling in a local sales environment, you could set the follow-up to be a quick drop-in. You might be thinking to yourself ... what if the advertiser wants to call me back and they refuse to set the follow-up? At that point, I believe you need to acknowledge the circumstance as it has been laid in front of you. I would ask this question: "If this is a marketing idea that you love I would think a follow-up would make a ton of sense, right? If this is not an idea that you love and you're just being kind to me, please let me know. My goal here is to help and not to be a waste of your time."

STRATEGY #4: Texting may be the best way to follow up. Ugh. Yes, I said it. I consider myself to be a technology expert. I absolutely love technology. I believe that technology has really helped salespeople increase our sales games and be more productive. But I admit that I am not a huge fan of texting clients.

The reason is because of the personal nature of texting. However, with that said, I have definitely seen a large majority of my clients move to texting as a quick way to follow up. To that end, at the close of a sales call, I want to make sure that I get the advertiser's permission to text them. Sure, you probably don't need to do this, but I just like to have someone's permission before I'm texting to their personal cell phone. Call me old-school if you want. I will wear it with a badge of honor. But please understand, I do recognize that texting is an important part of the sales process.

STRATEGY #5: Be safe, but recognize that face-to-face is still the best way to sell. My comments are not meant to be political in any way. I want everybody to be safe, and as a survivor of COVID-19, I would never wish it upon my worst enemy. I'm finding that most advertisers I'm working with are fine with face-to-face meetings. But be safe out there. Because it is hard to ignore that face-to-face meetings are better than virtual meetings. And yet we know that virtual meetings are always better than phone meetings.

So whatever you need to do out there, be safe, but recognize that getting in front of advertisers is a very important part of being a professional in the sales business. It is harder for an advertiser to ghost you after they have a personal, face-to-face conversation and connect with you.

STRATEGY #6: Present ideas on the spot. I have preached about this for years. You are not selling a cure for cancer. You are selling and recommending marketing options. So why are you not going to the sales call armed with a proposal filled with great ideas? Because someone has convinced you that you cannot create a proposal until you know the advertiser's "needs." This is just not true. In my world of media sales... any given advertiser in any given category is going to normally do three to six things to be successful. Period. So look at the past success other advertisers have had in a certain category and make educated recommendations. While on the sales call, tweak what you brought to better fit the advertiser's needs. There is truly no reason to leave to create a proposal. This is an invitation to be ghosted. Why give that invitation?

If you're a reader of my columns or listener of my podcast on a regular basis, you'll know that I'm all about having an organized sales plan of attack. I do like to be a little unorthodox at times, though, because breaking up consistent patterns of failure is very important to success. But still, never forget that failing to plan is planning to fail. And I believe that in the sales business, this quote is more accurate than ever.

In closing, ghosting is just something that's going to occur in the sales business. It's a part of the sales process. Be prepared for it. Any plan is better than no plan at all.

***

Chapter Thirteen: Time Management for Sales Success

Here are some shocking time management statistics and facts from Timezy.com:

• Of eight telephone calls placed, one will be repeated due to missing information.

• The average manager spends three hours per day handling unforeseen interruptions and problems.

• Employees, on average, work the hardest from 9 a.m. to 12 p.m. After this time, productivity tends to drop significantly.

• If you spend 10-12 minutes planning your day, you'll save up to two hours of time that would have otherwise gone to waste.

• The average person has tried and/or uses 13 different methods for managing their time.

• A typical office worker checks their email 50 times and their social media platforms 77 times per day while they're at work.

- It's proven that 66% of people check their emails seven days a week. They also expect to receive email responses the following day.

- Harvard University did a study and found that American companies lose roughly $65 billion due to their employees suffering from a lack of sleep.

- Seventy percent of people use a to-do list to ensure that they get all their most important tasks done.

- New ideas, concepts, and suggestions will be criticized in under 8 seconds.

- When it comes to planning allotted time for tasks, we underestimate how long a task will take almost every time. Most tasks take twice as long as we think.

- Those who work at a messy or otherwise unorganized workspace spend an hour and a half (on average) looking for misplaced items.

- Full-time employees generally work 8.5 hours per day, Monday-Friday, and 5.4 hours per day on the weekend.

- Workers receive, on average, seven to eight disruptions per hour. This equals 50-60 per day--most of which are unnecessary.

- Of every 10 people who attend a meeting, nine will daydream during it.

- Every day in America, there are roughly 17 million meetings.

- Florida State University discovered that a worker's performance peaks when they work uninterrupted for 90 minutes.

- Nearly half of all employees in America believe that meetings are the number one source of wasted time at the office.

- Employees spend, on average, 31 hours per month in meetings. This means that they spend an hour per day.

- Of the time given to a workday, 80% is spent doing tasks with little to no value and only 20% is spent doing something important.

- Within the last 20 years, the time that a person works has increased by 15%, while the same person's personal time decreased by 33%.

- A person who gives themselves one thing to do in a day will generally take all day to do it. If the same person gives themselves two things to do, both will get done. If someone adds 12 tasks to a to-do list, most people do not get all 12 done, but will get at least seven done.

- Sixty-two percent of full-time workers report work-related aches and pains, with 38% reporting pain in the hands, 44% eyestrain and pain, and 34% difficulty sleeping due to stress.

The time management statistics above show how effective adequate time management is. It also proves how important it is for the success of both companies and their individual employees. Without time management techniques, companies suffer from lost productivity, loss of revenue, and an increase in health deterioration among employees. If you take care of the minutes, the hours will really truly take care of themselves.

So let's look at how to do more with less, and how to become a focused, time management Ninja. I once heard Tony Robbins say something quite insightful. He said one reason that so few of us achieve what we truly want is that we never direct our focus. We never concentrate our power. Most people dabble their way through life and through work. They never decide to master anything.

Here's an example. I was in Palm Springs, California, teaching a class on nearly this same topic. All of a sudden as I was teaching, I realized I had a crazy kind of headache coming on. And this headache had actually been coming on for three or four days. It just wouldn't go away. It would come back and go away and come back. And finally one of my friends said, "Ryan, you know what you need to do? You're kind of crazy-busy, your schedule is mad, and you need to go to the doctor, because maybe something's wrong." Now come on, I was thinking. I'm just a red-blooded American guy. I'm like, "Nah." But I went to the doctor, and to my surprise I was rushed to the emergency room. And when I woke up, there was this face staring directly into my eyes. I thought to myself and I even said aloud, "Am I in heaven?"

And this really nice lady said, "No, you're in the emergency room and I'm your doctor." She said, "Mr. Dohrn, your blood pressure was up to 211 over 147." And she added, "I'm not sure that you died, but you got pretty darn close. Tell me, what do you do for a living?" And I said, "I travel 15 days a month. I sell, I speak to groups, you know, pretty normal stuff." And she said, "That's not normal at all. As your doctor, I need to advise you ... you need to get control of your life, and you need to get control of your schedule."

Fellow salespeople, I'm hoping you'll never have to end up in the emergency room before you make changes to your life. Here's what's funny, or at least interesting, about time. In 1860, there were 24 hours in a day. In 2016, there were 24 hours in a day. And I've not seen that there's any type of technology on the horizon that's going to give us more time in our day. In 2050, there will be 24 hours in the day. So I'd like to share with you several ideas, ones that can help you do more with less. We're all having to do it. So what do we do?

Time Management Idea #1: Prioritize ruthlessly. Why is it so important? It's important because what drives your daily agenda is really controlled by you. Sure, there are things in your office that are completely out of your control. People stopping by your office, a boss asking you for some type of crazy report, maybe a random phone call here or there. But here's what I have observed. I have the opportunity to coach some 500 people a year. And I've noticed that the most common thing that drives people's day is their email, their inbox, it's like we're under a mind control thing. Our daily agendas are driven by what happens in our inbox by people we may not even know. Even spammers distract our day. So for you, what's driving your daily agenda? Is it your email inbox? Or is it your priorities?

How many of us, at one time or another, have kept a written to-do list? A lot of us have, but we've got to recognize that the to-do list doesn't go with you on the bus, to the beach, to the bathroom, or to the bar. But guess what does? It's right there in your pocket... your phone. One of the best things about that device, although it, too, is a distractor, is that it allows you to keep track of your tasks and even to stay on task.

What I do each morning, first thing, is I open up my phone. I look at my task list, and I use that task list to keep me on track. What's interesting is that time management experts now tell us that a written to-do list kind of makes you feel good because you're able to work along and cross a few things off your list. But that list doesn't buzz, it doesn't flash. It doesn't go with you to the bathroom, on the bus, or to the beach.

So you've got to ask yourself, what can I do to be a time management Ninja? The first thing is to become amazing at prioritizing and keeping up with your tasks. It's so easy to pick up your phone and say, "Hey Siri, add a reminder to call Bob Jones tomorrow." "Hey Siri, I need to get that report complete. Set me a reminder for tomorrow." So, time management experts are now telling us to use that device... to use our smartphones. Every one we've got, whether Android or iPhone, all of them have a task management tool. Some will sync up with your software at work.

So I'd suggest that you should start each and every day with a session prioritizing your tasks. It might

182 • SELLING FORWARD

only take 10 seconds. It's one of the first things I do every day. It guides my day. My inbox doesn't guide my day. My task list guides my day.

Time Management Idea #2: Avoid random patterns. If there's one thing I know for certain, we never want to be the king or queen of Random Land. Randomness does not produce repeatable patterns of success. And that's what we're looking for, in life, in love, and with our families... repeatable patterns of success.

Consider this. There are maybe about five things that randomly occur that are actually good for us. Those five good things that randomly occur might be winning the lottery, finding money, getting a call from a good friend, a client calls from 2 years ago and buys from you, or maybe your best pal stops bye to say hello. All great things. All random.

If we really think about it, though, it's actually pretty difficult to come up with five things that randomly occur in our lives that are good for us. And that's because randomness kills our days. Randomness kills our momentum. Randomness kills almost everything that we do. So there are three things that I do to avoid random patterns that waste my time. Number one, I look for repeatable patterns of success. What are things that I do every day that produce a positve result? What are things that I say every day that work? What are emails that I write that work? What are subject lines that I use that work? I'm looking for repeatable patterns of success. And the reason I'm looking so deeply is because I know that when I see successful people, they're not random. Now, maybe they do things that are spontaneous, but randomness will kill your day. So look for repeatable patterns of success, write them down, and repeat them in your life. If you say something to your spouse, and it works, repeat it. If you ask your boss a question at a particular time of day, and you get an amazing response, repeat it.

Similarly, though, I want to be looking for patterns that don't work—looking for things in my life that are not giving me the result that I need. I recognize that some of us are always looking to work smarter and not harder. But good luck with that. Typically, nothing in life that's worth a darn is going to be given to us, or is going to come to us easily. Typically, before every great achievement, there's pain, and this is true before every great reward. So I want to identify things that are not working. And I want to create a little plan to get those things out of my life.

Here's one more important consideration as it relates to random patterns: always be looking. I want to look and find things that work and repeat them. Just as I want to find things that don't work, and I want to get those things out of my life as quickly as possible.

Time Management Idea #3: Create time blocks. Time blocks are vividly important. I talk about this when I'm teaching management classes and I talk about it when I'm teaching sales classes. You've got to create time blocks, because either you're going to control your calendar or someone else is going to control your calendar. Time blocking is just recognizing the things that I have to do every day, in the normal course of doing my job, that I can time block and create repeatable patterns of solid success.

Here's the thought I get when my alarm clock goes off. First off, I'm not really happy about it. And then I realize when my feet hit the floor that there are four or five things that I need to do. These are things that I have to do every day as a part of my daily job, no matter the job. What I'm going to do is I'm going to time block those things. I'm going to time block the things that I have to do so that people won't book meetings on my calendar. Remember, I don't want people to control my calendar. So I'm looking for things that I can actively repeat.

So now, when my alarm goes off in the morning, I have some comfort in the fact that I already know a few things in it that are repeatable every work day, and there's comfort in that structure. Would you be surprised to know that most people crave structure? Most successful children that graduate from high school, when you look back on their activities, you see that their lives were structured. Sure, you can be a helicopter parent and over-structure everything. Sure, we can time block the whole day and then become more stressed out. But what I find is kids that are raised with structure, teams that are built around structure, sales teams that have processes like time blocking, they're always more successful. It goes back to my point about not being random. Time blocking helps drive our activities forward.

Time Management Idea #4: Creating email templates. I remember when email wasn't around, and you might remember that, as well. But then again, I remember eight track tapes. So I remember when we would sell without email. We would just pick up the phone and call. And people would oftentimes pick up or they'd actually call us back. But now email is a part of our lives.

After learning from experience in my own sales life, here's how I handle email to see the best results. Any time I've written an email that's more than two times, I'm going to create a template for it. If you've done it twice, you're probably going to use it again. Then, I'm using email technology to my advantage. Email templates help me do more, with less work. Let me give you a few examples. You probably don't even know where to store templates in your email program. The two most common email programs people use are Outlook and Gmail. Inside of Outlook, you can save your templates two different ways. In Outlook begin by composing a message. Once you start that email, a template option is available under the message tab. Copy, paste, or write the email you want to save as a template.   In Gmail, I like to use canned responses. Canned responses allow me to save any of the responses that I'm going to have that are in the can. You can find canned responses under the settings under tabs and turn it on.

One other important thing with email as a sales tool ... you've got to recognize it if you're not good with grammar and spelling. Do not forget to use spell check or pay for Grammarly®. Trust me, it will be money well spent.

Time Management Idea #5: Turn off your email pop up. Turn it off. Turn off your email's ability to vibrate your phone that's in your pocket, as well. You might be thinking, "I could never do that. I have to give awesome customer service." But I'm not asking you not to give amazing customer service. I'm just asking you not to be a slave to your email. Just think about this. How much time do you potentially waste by thinking that you can answer an email really fast? But you must be aware of the 30-second interruption. What does that mean? Here's an example. You're writing a report and you hear 'ding" and you look down as an email comes in. Your brain says, "I can handle that real fast and be right back on task." That's a lie. Recognize that it's a lie. This little 30-second interruption can cause you to take two to four minutes to reengage and come back to the task.

How many times have you gone on to answer an email and then realized that you never got back on task? Now think about this. If you had 20 interruptions per day, that means you could be losing 40-60 minutes per day. That's 174 hours per work week that you can control just by not being distracted.

Consider this, too, if you're someone who thinks you've got to answer every email in a flash. I had an entire room of Millennials in front of me in one of my training classes, and I asked them, "If you send me a normal email in the course of a normal business day, how quickly do you want me to respond?" I was amazed at their answer, because Millennials were born with a cell phone in their hands. And they said, "Within twenty-four hours is fine." It's never going to take me 24 hours to respond to an email, but I am always going to respond promptly, just not instantaneously. Because when you're a slave to your inbox, you could be losing 174 hours per work year. That's like three weeks of work. You're welcome. I just gave you a three-week vacation right there. Think about it. If you make, say, 30 bucks an hour, it's costing you six grand a year. If you're making 60 bucks an hour, it's costing you $12,000. And what if you're someone who makes really good money? Consider that in 174 hours at $225 an hour, the email time drain I described is costing you $30-$40 thousand dollars a year.

So I'll say it again, email templates will save you so much time and keep you on task. Knowing your technology is so unbelievably important. Here's another thing that I do. In my brain, I recognize when an email comes into my inbox, I say to myself, is this a barn-burner? Is it a priority one, priority two, or priority three? Priority one emails I'll answer quickly, within an hour or so—but not instantaneously. Priority two, those are people that are important. I've got to get back to them within a couple of hours. Priority three, I'm always going to answer them before the end of the day. You've got to ask yourself: How do I prioritize these emails?

Time Management Idea #6: Schedule time for re-search in everything that we do, whether we're trying to find a hotel venue, a new piece of software, or just trying to find a way to become more productive. We've got to schedule time for research. If we don't, research happens at random times. And so because of that, we're letting that randomness, once again, control the day. We all have things that we need to do. So, as you think of these things, add them to your task list, then have a time block set aside for client re-search, or personal research and development for yourself. I dedicate at least one hour every single week, and I'm religious about it, to doing this type of research and development. Typically, it's going to be a Friday afternoon, sometime between 3:30 p.m. and 5 p.m. That's when I'm doing my personal research and development. If I don't set the time aside, no one's going to set it aside for me.

Time Management Idea #7: Become a technology ex-pert. Some of you are pretty darn good with your phones, and that's awesome, but were you aware that Outlook can do about 150 things for you, besides simply reply to email? Were you aware that there's well over 1,000 apps that you can add on to your Gmail to make yourself more efficient? As an example, there's a tool called If No Reply in Gmail. And with it you can actually set up five emails to go and sequence through Gmail, and if someone responds, it will stop the sequence. There are so many different ways that salespeople can potentially use that. I love the Gmail tool called Boomerang. Boomerang allows me to write an email to my brother or to a business client. And if they don't reply within a certain period of time, it boomerangs back to me and it pops to the top of my inbox. It's the easiest 19 bucks I spend each month. Speaking of calendars, I use a tool called Calendly. Calendly allows me to use my Google calendar to be able to give other people access to my calendar, so they can book time slots there. I love the fact that I've got a lot of help in my office, that I've got a great team. But one of the things that's hard for me to coordinate is my schedule. I'll send that Calendly link, people can click on it and see when I'm available, and I can control it and customize it. And I have basically eliminated a person being involved in that process by just using this simple tool.

If you use a CRM, become a technology expert there too. If you're on a Mac, did you know that you can click the function button twice and the dictation tool will automatically pop up, and you can just talk into your computer and it will write emails for you or put notes in your CRM? On a PC you press Windows H for the same dictation tool. It's awesome and it saves me so much time.

Time Management Idea #8: Create a process for everything that you do. Everything in life, in love, and in work and projects, you have to create a process for everything that you do. If you don't, what you're going to find is that you're constantly reinventing the wheel. It's painful. It's stressful. It's not efficient. How do you handle sales leads when they come in? How do you handle marketing leads when they come in? How do you reply to emails that you receive? When do you reply? How do you reply to meeting requests? How long do you work on something before you go and ask for help? All of these things require processes if you're to be successful.

Google calendar is an example of a tool that's in my process, reminding me of everything that I need to do.

I never miss a birthday, because I use technology to my advantage. I have a process. When I come home from being on a trip, and my awesome wife of 27 years has been running that house, I don't come in there and make it my own. It's her house, I come in and follow her rules. That's a process. That's why I think we've survived 27 years. And I know it sounds slightly overwhelming, like really ... a process for everything? I have so many processes in place that when I get stressed, when things aren't going well, I just fall back on that process. What are three things you need a process for right now? Declare the things. Then, create a process.

Time Management Idea #9: Set time limits for everything that they do. If you need to work on a proposal, then first determine how many minutes you think it will take. Let's say, 20 minutes, and set your phone timer and press go. I find that I actually respond better when I'm on the clock. When I'm under the gun like that, I always work better and I'm more efficient. Setting a timer for myself also allows me to say to somebody who might knock on my door, "Hey, I've only got five minutes left to get this done. If you don't mind, I'll get back to you in five minutes." I do this so often that people who come by my office will actually look at the phone on my desk to see how long they should wait before they come back. I've trained them. This formula is proven. According to Toggl, the time-tracking website, you can increase your productivity 150% just by setting time limits, So just by setting time limits, I'm increasing my productivity. No, some of you might not respond to a clock that's ticking down. In your mind you see a bomb about to go off. If that is the case, either add more time to clock or do not follow this advice.

Time Management Idea #10: Share your time management goals with your colleagues and your team. If you love these ideas, you're going to have to present them to your team. People abusing your time is often about them not understanding what you are trying to do. If people are constant vampires of time, just sucking time out of your day, they clearly don't know the goals that you're trying to achieve. They're on their agenda. They're on their schedule, because they don't know what you're trying to do. So you want to meet with your manager, or meet with your team, or meet with your boss or your spouse or whomever it is, and explain, "Hey, this is what I'm trying to do. This is my goal from a time management perspective. I'm going to ...

Number one, prioritize ruthlessly. Number two, I'm going to avoid random patterns. Number three, I'm going to create time blocks and block time for everything. Number four, I'm going to create email templates (remember, never write an email more than twice without creating a template for it). Number five, I'm going to turn off that ding on my phone, because it's costing me thousands of dollars a year. Remember, it's okay not to answer instantaneously. No one's going to die. Very rarely do emergencies come into your email. Number six, schedule time for research. Number seven, become a technology expert. Number eight, create processes for everything that you do. Number nine, set time limits for everything. And then last but not least, number 10: You've got to explain these goals and what you're working to accomplish to those you manage and to those around you.

Stephen Covey, author of "The 7 Habits of Highly Successful People," wrote in one of his books that the key is not spending time, but investing in time management. Do you know who said this, "Let our advanced worrying become advanced thinking and planning"? Winston Churchill said that. And Jim Rohn, who we've all known and loved for many years, said time is more valuable than money. Pay attention. Time is more valuable than money. You can get more money. You're never going to get more time.

***

Chapter Fourteen: Staying Mentally Strong During Tough Times

Exploring the intersection of mental health and sales fatigue is vital to reaching peak sales success in today's pandemic world.

Mental health is a very important subject for us to discuss as it relates to our work life and, I believe, our sales lives, as well. Please understand that I am not a clinically trained therapist in any way, shape, or form. I do hold an Associate Certified Coach (ACC) certification from the International Coaching Federation. My intention in this chapter is to provide inspiration to those of you who might have found yourselves in a sales rut or mentally fatigued at work, or in life, as we're getting back to some level of normal sales business across America. If you are experiencing significant mental fatigue or issues related to your mental well-being, please seek professional advice. I have listed several resources at the end of this chapter, which I dedicate to my fellow media sales warrior, Chris Atkins, who took his life amidst a vibrant media sales career. Chris, you are missed.

The National Institute of Mental Health reports that 31% of survey respondents report symptoms of anxiety or depression, 13% report having started or increased substance use, 26% report stress-related symptoms, and 11% report having serious thoughts of suicide within the past 30 days. These numbers are nearly double the rates expected before the pandemic. Friends, this is a real problem. This is more than a revenue issue. This is a human issue.

We've all had those days and weeks and months. Days when you just don't feel like doing much of anything, much less selling. It doesn't matter if you are selling copy machines or advertising. Some days you just don't feel like doing it. Have you had one of those days? If you haven't, you've probably not been selling for very long, because it's quite normal to feel this way. But know this: you are not alone out there.

So, what do you do? Is there a way to get yourself out of a sales rut? Is there a way to push through the mental fatigue? The answer is a resounding ... YES! Rather than blaming this dilemma on the pandemic, it's probably better for all of us in sales land to recognize that we're just normal people that have chosen a career many would never take for any amount of money. Each month I end my Ad Sales Nation podcast by saying, "If ad sales was easy, everybody would be doing it. And they're not. We are the chosen few. But, we've found a career that will feed our families for a lifetime." It is a statement that I feel deeply about. I tell my ad sales coaching clients all the time that I go where I want, eat where I want, travel where I want, all because of media sales. It has literally been a part of my life for 30 years. But over that period of time there have been many days, many weeks, many months when I've just not felt like I wanted to sell anything. Here are the seven things that I often do when I find myself in a sales rut or mentally exhausted from the business of sales.

1.   Connect with others in the sales business. The first thing for every sales rep to recognize is that sales ruts are normal and they happen to everybody. You are a unique person, but this circumstance and situation is not unique at all. You're human. These things happen to all of us. It's important also to surround yourself with other people that understand where you're coming from.

Oftentimes, those around you can't sympathize very much because they don't really know what it's like to be in the sales business. Think about it. If every day you're guaranteed a paycheck, you're not used to what we in sales land are going through each day. Being in sales is tough. We live and die by our sales activity. Nothing is a guarantee in sales. Having a few mutual connections that are also in the sales business is important to your long-term sanity. While it's always good to get other people's outside perspectives, it's also equally important to surround yourself with other people who completely and utterly understand what you're going through on a daily basis. There's a reason that people crinkle their noses when you tell them you are in sales. You probably do not smell bad. They just know they could not handle being in sales. In every major city there are groups of sales professionals that gather together on a regular basis. With COVID restrictions somewhat loosened across the country, It's probably easier now than it has been in the last year to find a group of like-minded sales professionals that you can gel with and who will provide you a shoulder to lean on. Here is a link to several groups that you can join: https://jobstars.com/sales-professional-associations-organizations/. I truly feel this is an important piece of the puzzle. If you're not able to find a networking group, seek out professional sales coaching. Finding a coach that's also in the sales business can be extremely helpful to you since they will be able to better sympathize with your current situation and provide guidance.

2.   Change your frequency. If you've ever had the opportunity to read the book The Secret, you'll understand a little bit of what I'm talking about. Even if you feel that book to be complete hocus-pocus, I feel it to be based in some level of reality. There is a universal understanding that when you continue to do something the same way and expect a different result, you are defining or trying to redefine the non-clinical version of insanity. Many of the salespeople that I personally coach will find themselves on the wrong frequency. They have been doing the same thing over and over again and expecting a different result, and they just can't see why things aren't going in their direction. Whether you believe that life operates on

certain planes or frequencies is completely up to you. But, I can tell you that changing things up, changing your frequency, can be part and parcel to your success in getting out of a sales rut. Recently, I was working with a fantastic sales professional that found herself in a sales rut. I encouraged her to change things up. To leave home at a different time for work. To drive a new direction to the office. To listen to a different style of music on her way to work. To change her coffee. To park in a different parking spot. To wear a different type of outfit than she would normally wear to work. All of these little factors contribute to you looking at things from a different perspective. What's interesting is that we are all creatures of habit. Some of those habits become so ingrained in our lives that even though we're doing the same thing over and over again, we just don't see it as being that simple. After just 48 hours of doing things completely differently than she normally would, she closed a big dollar sales deal. Was it the coffee? Was it a magic parking spot? No. I don't think that this is a conspiracy theory by any means. A lot of times it's just about retraining your brain to see things from a little bit of a different perspective. Try something different today. You might be surprised at how impactful it is on your life.

3.　　　　　Call a client who loves you. All of us have advertisers that we love. In some cases, I've been in the wedding of some of my favorite clients. After all, sales is about quality relationships with quality people. Do I love all my advertisers? The answer is ... no, I don't. But I do have a select group of advertisers and clients that I absolutely enjoy and would spend time with regardless of whether or not they did business with me. These are the types of people that I often call on when I'm having a bad day. I do not usually tell them that I'm having a bad day. But I will engage in conversation with them knowing that they are not going to beat me up about price or frequency or Facebook. There are three things that can come from this. The first is that you just might find a sales opportunity. The second is that you are actually doing yourself a favor by retaining that customer. The third is that you created a positive conversation that will probably lead to another one. I'm not suggesting that you ask your advertisers to be your therapist. I'm merely suggesting that when you talk to people that really like you, you tend to re-energize yourself with positivity.

4.   Work your list of clients. Within any competent CRM system, you are able to form a list of customers. I have three lists that I work on a daily basis. The first list is a standard prospecting list like the one we all have in front of us. The second list contains those clients that I've already met with that I consider "in progress" towards a sale. The third list is my active clients that I am looking to retain for a lifetime. When I'm having a bad sales day, I focus on my lists. I might put on some rock music and increase the strength of my coffee, and then I work my lists. What I find is that lists create focus. When you're mentally fatigued you often have a hard time focusing. With a focused list, I'm able to really laser-focus in on a particular group of people that I'm calling for a reason. Keep in mind, I'm not a big fan of leaving voice messages and asking people to call me back. Rather, I leave a voicemail to encourage a customer to reply to the email that I sent. So, when I'm working this list, I am usually using a cadence of phone calls

first, followed up by an immediate email. My lists are a living, breathing document. My goal is not to work a list from 10 to 0. My goal is to have a list that is always growing and changing. From a pipeline sales management perspective, I never want any of my lists to get to 0. If your CRM system can't create a list, I would suggest you find a new CRM.

5.   Work new categories. In addition to the list that I work on a daily basis, I will oftentimes change my sales approach on categories that I sell. Personally, I like to trade accounts with other sales professionals on my team. The reason for this is because when I give someone an account that I've worked hard and they trade with me, we almost always close a deal one way or the other. Many times customers just need to hear a different tone of voice or a different approach. From a team perspective, I like the fact that I can get out of a certain category and focus on another category to give my brain something fresh to look at.

6.   Get some sleep. Sleep experts from the Mayo Clinic tell us that a lack of focus or mental fatigue can often be traced back to a lack of sleep.

Don't fool yourself. Most adults need seven or more hours of sleep each night to function at a high capacity level. If you're like most salespeople, after a long day you'll have a couple of cocktails, a nice meal, and stay up late binge-watching Netflix. Completely normal. But also, this particular habit could lead you to a lack of sleep. One of the things I noticed when I was diagnosed with sleep apnea is that I was definitely not getting enough sleep. I am an eight-hours of sleep kind of guy. My body truly needs eight hours of sleep. Can I function on seven hours of sleep? Absolutely. But if I want to be at my prime, I need eight hours of sleep. I know this sounds like a basic thought. Sort of a 101 kind of thing, right? So do it! Sometimes it does take a village to be successful. You may need to talk to your significant other and make it a team effort. In the end, though, your success is a team success at home and in the office.

7. Get back to the basics. When things aren't going well it is a common practice for us to take random sales approaches to see what might stick against the wall. This is an absolutely bad sales strategy whether you're new or old in the sales

business. There are fundamental pieces to the sales game that have to be achieved in order for you to be successful. Go back to the basics. Are your emails short and simple and to the point? Are your emails and voice mails relevant to the exact needs of the customer? Are you contacting your customers at the optimal time of day? Are you selling strictly on the phone or are you trying to get in front of people to have face-to-face meetings? These are just a few of the basics that you need to wrap your head around if you're going to be successful and get back on the sales horse for a long ride to victory. Look back at your sales life. What are the three things that worked best for you in the past? Go back and look at them closely.

In the end, you control you. While other people around you influence you ... in the end, the decisions that you make are the decisions that you will make. Please don't settle for the statement, "It is what it is." I don't accept that with myself or with my family members or with my team members. I truly believe it is what you make it.

If you're in a sales rut, choose just one of the seven ideas listed in this column and put it into action. Wrap your brain around it. Commit to it. And own it. Getting out of a rut is not about giving it half your effort. It's going to take everything you've got to get the train back on the tracks and rolling in the right direction.

And finally, never, ever be afraid to ask for help.

As I stated at the beginning, you might find yourself in a situation where you just can't get yourself mentally correct. Please seek professional advice if that happens. Here are some resources to help.

National Suicide Prevention Lifeline: Call 1-800-273-TALK (8255); En español 1-888-628-9454

Use Lifeline Chat on the web: https://suicidepreventionlifeline.org/chat/

The Lifeline is a free, confidential crisis service that is available to everyone 24 hours a day, seven days a week. The Lifeline connects people to the nearest crisis center in the Lifeline national network. These centers provide crisis counseling and mental health referrals.

<u>Crisis Text Line</u>: Text "HELLO" to 741741. The Crisis Text hotline is available 24 hours a day, seven days a week throughout the U.S. The Crisis Text Line serves anyone in any type of crisis, connecting them with a crisis counselor who can provide support and information.

One of my goals in writing this book and including this chapter was to give you some ideas to stay #SalesStrong!

***

Chapter Fifteen: Your Action Plan for Success

When it comes down to it, what will you do with the information in this book? Let's wrap up with the fundamental things that we need to do consistently every year—in sales, in marketing, and in business—to truly become and to stay exceedingly successful.

These suggestions go way beyond the standard New Year's resolutions people make. Because did you know that 75% of people just like you and me fail on those resolutions by January 28? They don't even keep those resolutions alive more than 28 days!

Why? It's because they don't do these 10 things to set themselves up for success—success that lasts all year long and takes them into the next.

No 1: Set keystone habits first.

Most people go straight to goal setting, when they really need to set keystone habits first. What are they? They are far more important than the big media sales goals you will set for 2021.

But what is a keystone? If you look at an arch in a doorway, picture an old castle if you will, there's a prominent stone right in the center that looks like a wedge or a piece of pie. It will resemble a triangle of sorts. And without that stone, called the "keystone," the arch would fall. The strength of that arch comes from the keystone right in the center. It's that foundational piece of an arch that's going to last hundreds, if not thousands, of years.

What are keystone habits for you and me? Simple things, like getting plenty of sleep. Drinking plenty of water. Reducing stress by getting out and exercising. Things like that.

Think about it this way. Is weight loss a keystone habit? The answer is probably no. But a keystone habit to help you reach that larger goal might be, when you're at the grocery store, to only shop from the outside aisles of the store, and not in the middle where the less healthy stuff is. Right?

Keystone habits are fundamental. What do they look like for you? The biggest one for me is sleep—making sure I get at least eight hours each night. And it's tough, because I love to binge watch Netflix after a long day of work.

So think about your keystone habits … they're going to be different from your big goals, but they're going to set you up for success so you can reach the big ones.

No. 2: As you're setting goals, identify the "why" in the goal.

Before you think about how you'll get to your sales goals you've got to think about why. The why is fundamentally important to your success in goal setting.

Going back to the weight loss example, what would the "why" look like? Why are you trying to lose weight? To be healthier. But why? To live longer. But really, why? So that you don't die! And you can actually enjoy the fruits of your labor.

So idea no. 2 gets down to the heart of the matter— and making sure you identify the "why" in every goal that you set. Not just the what, not just the how, but the why.

No. 3: Set mini goals to get to your bigger goals.

See, a lot of times the reason you fail on the big goals is because the mini goals have not been set or achieved. And there's typically three mini goals below each main goal. And when you actually achieve your mini goals, that allows you to get to your big goal.

So let's say, for example, that your big goal is to exceed your sales numbers. Excellent. Now what are the mini goals to get you there?

One mini goal might be to establish an active pipeline that you're working every three days. And perhaps that could start with even another mini goal—like learning how to work your CRM really effectively.

Another mini goal in trying to get to the bigger goal could be that you're going to learn your sales math, your call-to-close ratios, and then improve upon them.

To sum up: mini goals ... think of a ladder. You climb one step at a time to get to the top. Set mini-goals to get to your bigger goals. And before that? Establish your keystone habits, and then sit down and identify the "why" in your bigger goals.

No. 4: Become a time management master.

We're all being tasked to do more with less. So, being a time management master comes down, in my sales experience, to time blocking. You've absolutely got to learn to time block.

Let's say one of your mini goals is, "I need to call 25 people each and every day." How will you reach this? Time blocking. Put it on your calendar and make it repeat each day.

Time blocking is fundamentally one of the greatest things I've ever done that's made the most impact on my sales life, my marketing life ... even my personal life.

No. 5: Plan to adjust your plan.

Planning to adjust your plan is part and parcel to your success, because a lot of times we fail at goals simply because the train came off the tracks as we were trying to get to the goal. And when that happened, we simply didn't know what to do.

So, plan to adjust your plan. Just plan to fail. "WHAT?" you're saying. The gurus (be careful about self-proclaimed gurus) always say, "You've got to visualize winning. Visualize reaching your goals."

But here's what I tell people to think about in my sales training. Plan to fail so that you have a plan for when the train comes off the tracks—so you can get back on the tracks again, really fast. Planning to adjust your plan is really about understanding that the vast majority of people are going to fail on their way to getting to the big goal. So because of that, you want to plan to adjust your plan.

When the mini goal train goes off the tracks, how do you see that it's going off the tracks and how do you get it back on? A lot of it, quite honestly, is simply paying attention.

No. 6: Oftentimes, you will need an accountability buddy.

Think about it. When do you lose the most weight? When you have a buddy. When do you gain the most muscle mass—on your own or with a trainer? Usually with a trainer. You probably need some kind of an accountability buddy.

Now, if you don't have one, you can use your calendar, your phone, an app to constantly remind you. Whatever you use, an accountability buddy is vitally important in your sales life, your marketing life, and in your business life.

How do you find one? Maybe you pay for a coach. And that's okay—I have a coach, and I think I'm pretty good at what I do, but I have a coach. And that coach is always asking me, "How are you doing on this? How are you doing on that?"

Having an accountability buddy, in whatever form that takes for you, is very, very important.

No. 7: Know your sales match and your deal count.

In the sales business, if you're going to achieve your sales goals, you've got to know your deal counts. We spent an entire chapter on this in the book. Maybe re-read it? You've got to know your call-to-close ratios.

It's so difficult to go into a month of selling if you don't know how many calls you need to make to get a meeting. And then, how many meetings do you need to have to close a deal? And how many deals do you need to get to goal?

To be successful in the sales business, you've got to know your numbers so you know what it takes for you to close a deal. I stress this over and over in my sales training.

Here's an example. I know that if I call 10 people and I work them every three days, out of those 10 people I'm going to get a couple of meetings. Then, out of those meetings, usually about half of them, I'm going to get a proposal in front of that person. And from there, about 30% of the time I'm going to close.

So, when I get to 10 meetings, I close about three in 10. And I think that's very, very successful.

But I was talking to a guy the other day and he said, "Ryan, I close 80% of meetings I go on. So I need help closing that last 20%." And I'm like, "Dude, you need to write a book, because nobody closes 80% (without discounting)."

So, know your sales math and your deal count. I truly believe that if you're closing 30%, you're doing well out there in COVID sales land.

No. 8: Recognize randomness when it occurs, and get rid of it.

Randomness kills your day. Randomness kills your goals. Randomness will kill your love life. Randomness will kill your personal life.

Randomness does not help you win.

So how do you recognize it and how do you get rid of it? First, it's very simple. Look for things that work and repeat them. And then look for things that don't work, and don't repeat them.

I know it sounds so simple, but people just don't pay attention. Recognize things that work and repeat those things. Recognize things that are not working and stop doing them.

It's amazing to me the number of people that do the wrong thing in the sales business, in the marketing business, and in business in general. And they just keep doing it. I believe they think to themselves, "If I just work harder it's going to work out."

And I know where this comes from. It comes from having really great parents, grandparents, or some-body who raised you say, "If you work hard enough, you can achieve anything."

Well, there's some truth in that. I'm not trying to di-minish what your parents or grandma said to you, but recognize: When things aren't working, stop doing the things that don't work.

Conversely, when things are working, repeat the things that do work. Pay attention to them. Because these are the things that will make you successful.

No. 9: Set rewards for yourself if you need them.

Maybe your rewards look something like this, "I'm going to do this, and then if this is the end result I get a spa day for myself," or, maybe for you it's an expensive bottle of bourbon. Whatever that looks like for you, set rewards for yourself if you need them. For those of you that are sales leaders reading this book, celebrate victories no matter the size. There are a lot of smaller victories that lead to the big wins. Be sure to incentivize and celebrate all victories along that path towards great sales success.

No. 10: Work your plan.

In my sales training, I encourage people to have a whiteboard in their offices. And I encourage them to write down their mini goals and their goals, and then to track themselves. The reason is, you've got to work your plan.

What's your plan? Work it. If you're not working your plan, nobody else is going to work it for you.

***

Final thoughts... In Conclusion

I would like to conclude this book by saying thank you and by sharing some of my favorite business quotes.

1. "I never lose. I either win or learn." – Nelson Mandela

2. "The secret of getting ahead is getting started." – Mark Twain

3. "Faith is taking the first step even when you don't see the whole staircase." – Martin Luther King Jr.

4. "True nobility is being superior to your former self." – Ernest Hemingway

5. "Once you replace negative thoughts with positive ones, you'll start having positive results." – Willie Nelson

6. "A fool thinks himself to be wise, but a wise man knows himself to be a fool." – William Shakespeare

7. "Don't bother telling the world you are ready. Show it. Do it." – Peter Dinklage

8. "Once you lose your excuses, you will find the results you seek." - Andre' Marie Dohrn (Ryan's wife)

9. "I am hitting my head against the walls, but the walls are giving way." – Gustav Mahler

10. "If sales was an easy job, everyone would be doing it. And... they are not. We are the chosen few that have found a career that will feed our families for a lifetime. " - Ryan Dohrn

My hope is that this advice will help you take your sales life to places you only dreamed possible.

Thank you for reading. Thank you for your support.

Ryan

**More online at :
RyanDohrn.com**

CPSIA information can be obtained
at www.ICGtesting.com
Printed in the USA
LVHW081957250322
714086LV00017B/1831